Praise For *My Exuberant Voyage*

Norman Weissman's *My Exuberant Voyage* tells of a career filled with adventurous encounters with the historic events of his time. As a global documentary filmmaker, film and TV writer-director, and novelist, Weissman has tales to tell worth reading. The author speaks with authority, intelligence, and with a clear moral compass, bears witness to history. A good read from an engaged writer.

Richard Geller
Author of: *The Raspberry Man*

Riveting portraits of the fascinating people Weissman encountered in his long career, and insightful accounts of events that shaped contemporary America and the 20th century world.

As in his earlier exposé of the Kent State shootings, *Snapshots USA*, Weissman once again reveals the strengths and virtues of his subject as well as hard truths some historians prefer to ignore.

Altogether the experiences he recaptures in these masterfully written essays clarify our understanding of turning points in our time, and ultimately renew our faith in the future of civilization.

My Exuberant Voyage is the author's optimistic summing up of who we are and what we can become.

William J. Kelly
Author of: *The Basilisk Solution*

Norman Weissman's career as a documentary filmmaker took him all over the world where he encountered the best and worst tendencies of our troubled human race. In *My Exuberant Voyage*, the author looks for, and finds, the idealism, courage and resilience that makes the survival of our civilization possible. A hopeful work of memory filled with many vital lessons from our past. Three cheers!

Forrest Stone, Playwright
Author of: *No Signs Allowed After This Sign*

My Exuberant Voyage
(A Witness To History)

Norman Weissman

All rights reserved under International
and Pan American Copyright Conventions.

Published in the United States by
Hammonasset House Books LLC
64 Edgecomb Street
Mystic, CT. 06255

Catalogue in Publication Data is available from
Library of Congress Control number: 2009911367

ISBN-13: 978-0-9801894-3-8

FICO: 14000

www.hammonassethouse.com

Cover Photo: Seymour Weissman © 2009

Printed in the United States of America

For my children:

Brian, Joel, Stephanie, Rebecca, Adrian and Joshua,
the golden threads of love and joy in my life.

PROLOGUE

I.B. Singer, a Polish-American novelist wrote: "Every writer must have an address. A place where his soul lives."

Certainly my address was created not only by the people I encountered, but by the books impacting my mind, the teachers mentoring me, and the friends and family encouraging my efforts to be whatever I might possibly become.

My address is comprised of successes and failures, dreams and fears energized by some inexplicable center around which my life revolved.

On my thirteenth birthday I received a portable Royal typewriter. Keys to the interior Kingdom of my mind. I soon became a prolific "hunt and peck" writer of school reports, letters to friends and family, and stories now lost to all but memory. Those early years at the keyboard never brought me enlightenment or revelation, but there did begin a lifetime process of discovering what I thought by writing. Finding words that not only expressed my thoughts, but revealed the emotions underlying them.

And so an inquiring boy became a man who did his best thinking while struggling to write what he thought. Refining a sense of truthfulness became my path out of personal chaos. An often futile attempt to bring my inner darkness out into the light where I could confront who and what I am. Where I lived. What my true address is.

At eighty-four, striving to see the world with sighted eyes and a feeling heart, and witnessing the truth of Tennessee William's observation "that the syllable of Time is Loss," I am aware of my personal race against Time. I fear not the loss of my physical being but rather the fading of my ability to focus and assemble complex thoughts. I think. I write. Therefore I am - is the essence of the life of the mind. To lose this would be to lose life itself.

However I am consoled by a firm belief I shall live in minds I have touched with my love. Love, the bridge between darkness and light, between being and non-being, between past and future, is eternal.

I love. Therefore I am. Forever.

And so I shall begin with a quotation defining what a memoir should be.

"A memoir is a work of sustained narrative prose that, though it originates in actuality and not invention, bears the same responsibility as does all writing to shape a piece of experience, transform a set of events, deliver a bit of wisdom. The reader must always be persuaded that the narrator is speaking the truth, and that he or she is honestly working hard to get to the bottom of the experience at hand in order to better understand one's own self. A novel has many agendas, a memoir only one – self definition. The question being asked in an exemplary memoir is: who am I? On that question the writer of a memoir must deliver. Not with an answer but with the depth of inquiry."

HAITI

The idea that the more things seem to change the more they remain the same has been confirmed by personal experience. From the Great Depression of my childhood to September 11, 2001 catastrophic events have left our nation fundamentally unchanged. America's courage, productivity, freedom and democratic character are as resilient as the Pyramids.

However the belief emerging from the wreckage of the World Trade Center, and dominating our media, that from this day forward everything will be different, ignores our country's remarkable ability to survive the disasters of war and peace with democratic institutions and national character intact.

Also unchanged are the world's intractable problems. The root causes of International Terrorism. Overpopulation, hunger, disease and illiteracy have never been substantially alleviated by dedicated Idealists who are called unrealistic do-gooders or bleeding hearts.

Creating a better World is a dream viewed as hopeless by Realists with little faith in Man's ability to change. Human frailty, Realists insist, determines

11

the circumstances of human life and to change Man's essential nature is impossible.

The eternal conflict between Idealists and Realists determined many critical choices. Such decisions as choosing One World or None. A choice emerging from the bloodbaths of two World Wars leading to the establishment of the United Nations at a time when such idealism was applauded and not disparaged by congress or the media. Hopefully, to paraphrase President Lincoln, the UN will someday prove to be the last best hope for Man on earth.

Benjamin A. Cohen, a 1950 recipient of the One World Statesmanship Award and Assistant Secretary General for the UN's Department of Public Information passionately believed in mankind's infinite possibilities of change. His faith in the United Nations' ability to change the dire circumstances of underdeveloped countries emerged from his childhood in Chile where he witnessed all the tragic problems of "Third World" nations. He focused the UN's search for a solution to conditions that were not just abstractions cited in the UN's Charter, but grim realities to be confronted and changed.

In 1951 the UN established the world's first Technical Assistance Program in Haiti's Marbial Valley. I had the good fortune to go to Haiti to research and write a documentary film script about this precursor of all Foreign Aid Programs addressing truly apocalyptic problems threatening life on earth.

Looking back more than fifty eight years I now realize I witnessed the first Act of an eternal conflict between Bleeding Heart Idealists and Practical Realists with the successful outcome of their cosmic struggle very much in doubt.

In 1951, Haiti was, and is today the world's most tragic "Basket Case". Three million people crowded into ten thousand square miles give Haiti the world's highest population density. Greater than China or India. The blacks and light-skinned Haitians have their racial roots in Africa and cultural roots in France. Only in geography is Haiti Caribbean. Governed by a minority of upper class Elites who do no manual labor, the 97 per cent majority are Peasants ministered by white French Catholic Priests or *Prêtre Savans*. Unordained Bush Priests. Haiti is cruelly divided by language, religion, and a rigid caste system that thwarts all possibility of reform.

From 1915 to 1934 Haiti was occupied by United States Marines who built the few rutted roads that survived in 1951. The Americans instituted the first Public Health measures coping with such epidemic diseases as Yellow Fever, Malaria, Hookworm, Small pox, Yaws, and Leprosy. For nineteen years American efforts at rural education were frustrated by a governing Elite who feared that with education Peasants would desert the land and no longer be subservient. Although French is Haiti's official language spoken by the Elite, everyone speaks Creole. The language of daily life and commerce.

In 1951 Jean Oser, a director at Warner Pathe's New York Studio assured me my imperfect French would enable me to understand Haiti's crude Creole variant and he insisted I would also benefit from hearing the elegant French spoken by the Elite, the world's most charming, cultured admirers of that "Universal Light of the World", French civilization. For Elite Haitians consider France their mother country and "The Declaration of the Rights of Man" their national birthright.

With this encouraging advice Jean Oser handed me a Pan American Airways ticket to Port Au Prince, three months expense money, and wished me luck.

Viewed from the air, Haiti's high mountains rising up out of the sea confirmed the accuracy of Christopher Columbus' letter to Queen Isabella describing the island as "Enchanting. A wonder of mountains and plains so beautiful and rich for planting and rearing cattle of all kinds, surpassing anything that would be believed by one who has not seen it."

However, looking out the window on final approach to Port Au Prince one sees a Haiti Columbus never could have imagined. Surrounding the airport a vast slum, a *bidonville* or Tin Can Village built of flattened kerosene cans, houses most of the city's population. Disembarking from the air-conditioned comfort of the plane into humid tropical heat I again discovered with my first breath the pungent odor of poverty and backwardness described to me by an American Diplomat as the characteristic smell of "The Turd World."

On the plane I read the UN report on Haiti describing thousands of once fertile acres ruined by desperate overuse and ignorant misuse. Haiti's once vast Tropical Forests were destroyed by land-hungry Peasants in need of farmland. Without trees to hold steep mountain slopes in place, the rich topsoil washed away by torrential rains silted up rivers and streams and flowed out to sea where the soil nourishes not even the fish.

My taxi from the airport was painted a kaleidoscope of dazzling colors of the most intricate designs decorating a battered 1938 Chevrolet. Roaring unmuffled through Port Au Prince's crowded streets, we blasted aside with a musical horn pedestrians, donkeys and street vendors who seemed indifferent to danger. As we drove through the great market square the scent of roasting coffee, the fragrance of brilliant patches of bougainvillea and hibiscus somehow, by their vivid beauty, mitigated this scene of depressing squalor.

Yet it appeared familiar. I was again seated in the Avalon Theater on Brooklyn's Kings Highway viewing a Biblical Epic. Noisy confusion everywhere. Hundreds of men, women and children buying and selling clothing, vegetables, live chickens, and other merchandise with tumultuous vitality. However instead of an ominous Hollywood movie scene I saw smiling faces and heard piercing cries and uproarious laughter as if each consummated transaction was a source of pure joy.

My dismay vanished as if the sun had come from behind a dark cloud spot-lighting this hustling crowd. I saw nothing but beautiful faces. All sizes. All shapes. Young. Old. Light, medium and dark-skinned people of color. Full of Life. Thriving despite poverty, hunger and rampant disease. I saw more vividly than ever before - The family of Man.

As we approached Oloffsons' Hotel, highly recommended by Pan American, we passed well-built, attractive homes of the Haitian Elite. Gated and enclosed by high garden walls, with iron shuttered windows and spacious verandas they seemed an urban sanctuary disconnected or unaware of the grim poverty of Port Au Prince. As the taxi drove off from Oloffsons I saw a hand lettered board in the rear window. Instead of a license plate the cab was identified by a name familiar to all lovers of classic French Literature. It was Heloise, the name of the recipient of the Poet Abelard's passionate letters to his beloved. In a few days I met another Abelard. Abelard Dessanclos. And the name of his passionate love was - Haiti.

Oloffson's Hotel deserved a reputation for romantic splendor. Enclosed inside a high-walled multi-colored tropical garden of tantalizing fragrance, the old Chateau was a remnant of Haiti's ostentatious colonial past when "wealthy as a Creole" described an Elite thriving on exports of sugar, coffee, indigo and cotton. In 1951, in the off-season of an impoverished Haiti, I was the hotel's only transient guest sharing the high-ceilinged dining room and spacious veranda with such permanent residents as exiled Royalty fleeing their East European homelands.

On the veranda that evening, at sunset, looking out over Port au Prince while enjoying the strong taste of Haitian Rum, I discovered the memorable beauty that exists beyond the overcrowded slum shanties of *bidonville*. Haiti's pervasive poverty and backwardness were for a moment forgotten as its spacious harbor bordered by cloud-covered mountains welcomed returning Fishing boats home from the sea. Gliding ghost-like across the water before the prevailing afternoon sea breeze, their tattered multi-colored sails were a picturesque Travel Brochure scene. The dismay I felt driving from the airport soon became the enchantment Christopher Columbus described. I was enthralled by this exotic land "surpassing anything that would be believed by one who has not seen it."

Max Seligman approached holding a tall Rum drink and sat beside me with the welcoming look of a compatriot meeting another American in a foreign land. He explained he was editor, publisher and reporter for The Haitian Sun the country's only English language newspaper. Max was one of many Americans "Hooked on Haiti". He loved everything about this impoverished land. After being unemployed for six months when New York's last liberal newspaper "PM" stopped publishing, he fled the Rat Race to find a better life for himself and family. Max now lived the great dream of all expatriates. Living in a tropical paradise in a spacious mansion with two servants, instead of enduring a crowded three-bedroom apartment in a New York City Housing project.

"What brings you to Haiti?" he asked. His distinct Brooklyn accent gentled by rum and a relaxed Caribbean life-style gave him the look of a seedy beachcomber in a Charles Laughton movie. He listened intently as I explained where I was going and what I would be writing about. "I wish you luck," he said. "I hope you are not too late."

"What's the problem?" I replied startled by his remark.

"Well the Marbial Valley where you're going is Haiti's 'Death Valley'," he replied, "where more Blacks die of disease and starvation than anywhere on the Island. For the *Gens du couleur*, the People of Color, the ruling Elite, the Marbial is a humiliation and the United Nations project calls attention to what is, for these charming cultured Haitians, an embarrassment."

"President Magloire invited the UN here."

"He did," Max said. "And a coal-black Army Colonel as President also humiliates the proud lighter-skinned Elite living in their beautiful *Petite Paris* by the sea."

"But the UN project is run by educated Haitians. Certainly they are from the Elite."

"Considered traitors to their class. People of color, the Haitian Elite, never have and never will do anything for the overwhelming black majority of the population. The UN is threatening a Caste system more rigid than India's. Teaching blacks to read and write Creole, the language they speak in this French cultural paradise, is futile. Confronting Haitian history is like pissing into the wind. The UN can't change an entire culture. The Elite will always fear what the blacks would do with a little education."

"Well," I said. "That's what I'm here to write about. If the UN succeeds in Haiti they can succeed anywhere in the world."

"Don't bet on it. The Church feels the UN threatens their hold on education which is really no education for the blacks who rarely speak French. The sooner the UN leaves Haiti the better. That's what the Bishop has been saying."

The next morning I visited the Haitian Culture Exposition built by Haiti's previous President Dumarsais Estimé to attract Tourists. Estimé, now exiled in Cuba with embezzled treasury funds, left as his legacy a handsome white Pavilion now housing the Tourism Minister's office.

The walls of the high-ceilinged hall were murals depicting Haitian history. Nothing I had seen in Mexico City's Diego Rivera murals portraying the events of their bloody revolution, or the Orozco murals at the Dartmouth College library depicting a returning Christ chopping down the Cross matched the shocking impact of these walls. The murals were a celebration of death. For on August 20, 1791 five hundred thousand abused plantation slaves revolted indiscriminately slaughtering every white man, woman and child in France's most prosperous colony. As a result of the accumulated hatred of a cruel century of French rule, white women were raped and their children disemboweled with machetes. The slaves revolt more than exceeded France's revolutionary Reign of Terror as Haiti's ravaged white population fled or were killed. The murals depicted every grisly horror. The violent blood red colors on mutilated bodies glorified the carnage accompanying the liberation and birth of the Haitian nation. The Hall commemorated a holocaust preceding Auschwitz's horrors by more than a century.

The murals also dramatized the ongoing conflict between the cultured French-speaking Elite and freed Creole-speaking blacks. A sharp division that still determines Haiti's tragic history. For Toussaint L'Ouverture, Haiti's first president, born a slave, was a military genius who defeated Napoleon's efforts to regain his prosperous colony only to have his great achievements betrayed by people of color who wanted to have slaves work their plantations. This never-ending struggle between blacks and *Gens du couleur* I realized, will decide the fate of the UN's Technical Assistance Program in Haiti. A daunting thought.

The next morning Army Sergeant Poisson parked his Jeep in Oloffson's driveway waiting to drive me to

Jacmel, a day-long hundred mile journey to a small town on Haiti's Southern coast. Here another Jeep or truck would bring me to the United Nation's Marbial Valley Compound. Sergeant Poisson greeted me with a firm handshake and a smile. Like many Haitians fleeing the drudgery of farming into the well-fed security of the Army, he acquired the commanding look of a soldier. As he secured my luggage on the back seat he explained with a hand gesture and a few words of French that our trip would probably be rough. As we drove from Port Au Prince on the route to Leogane I saw what he meant as we bounced along a highway constructed by US Marines during their 19 year occupation of Haiti. Not maintained since 1934, when the Marines departed, bone-shaking potholes and terrifying ruts were deepened and made permanent by years of neglect. Haitians can also thank the Marines for more than Medical Clinics or road-building, for Marines fathered many lighter-skinned Blacks elevating their status in Haiti's color-conscious Caste system. What was resented by Haitian blacks was the manifest American prejudice in favor of the light-skinned Elite who during and after the occupation held political power until the election of Colonel Paul Magloire, Haiti's first black President in sixteen years. Just before the town of Leogane we left the American built highway along the Bay of Gonave and turned onto a narrow track climbing up over the mountains to Jacmel, a small city on Haiti's southern Caribbean seacoast. No more than a widened footpath, our road followed a river occasionally crossing the shallow stream to drive along the banks and for many miles our Jeep travelled axle deep in water, a groaning sea-going mechanical monster charging into the unknown at three to five miles an hour. At each lurch or shocking blow to our tormented vehicle Sergeant Poisson laughed or shouted encouragement promising that in a few more miles the road would improve. That those few more miles never arrived in a few more hours was never mentioned as the good Sergeant enjoyed our bone-jarring journey. His good will was irrepressible. He even began to sing a little.

At noon we stopped, and under a blazing hot sun shared plantains and mangoes washed down with Taffin, raw Haitian Rum. After a few sips we agreed the road was a bad joke travelled by fools who seem to be under the protection of an all-forgiving Deity who protects drunks, children and American built Jeeps. For what else explains our survival?

With a personal bond now established I learned he had five children and a common-law wife, for in a holdover from slavery, marriage was dispensed with as an impediment to their Masters ability to sell their slaves. And so *Plaçage* rather than holy matrimony prevails, accepted and respectable, even among the lighter-skinned Elite who, with no disrepute, often have several such relationships.

Poisson had but one wife. His only other passion was painting. I had visited Peter DeWitt's Art Gallery in Port Au Prince and seen an astonishing collection of primitive Haitian Art purchased by tourists from visiting Cruise Ships. I was delighted by the painting's child-like vitality and colors, their native self-taught artists' imaginations inflamed by folklore and an intense religiosity. And Poisson now shyly confessed he was also a struggling *Peintre* whose work Critics say resembled Gauguin. An artist whose work he had never seen.

Jacmel's Hotel Excelsior was once the handsome residence of a departed wealthy Frenchman, and as Sergeant Poisson drove off for his return to Port Au Prince I marveled at his unquestioning acceptance of Haiti's neglected roads, fallen bridges, abandoned irrigation ditches, and burned-out Chateaus. Gone With the Wind would understate the devastation. It was as if maintaining or repairing any of the colonial infrastructure would be unpatriotic. A vote in favor of, or a nostalgia for, Haiti's tragic past under slavery. The Hotel Excelsior, where I was the only guest, was an exception to this rejection of all remnants of Colonialism. Two storey white-washed walls under a high-peaked Caribbean-style tin roof overlooked the harbor. *Le Propriétaire* a tall, light-skinned Elitist had the elegant manner of a Maitre de at New York's Four Seasons restaurant.

After showing me my room, assuming I shared all the expected white American prejudices, he assured me with a charming smile, "Pas de nègre ici. Jamais."

I nodded and replied "Je comprens, Monsieur. Je comprens," as if relieved to hear the good news about this all-white sanctuary in the world's oldest black Republic.

Dinner that evening would delight the most critical gourmand.

After an excellent wine and several demi-tasse cups of Haitian coffee, *Le Propriétaire* arrived at my table with a bottle of Cognac and offered a complimentary nightcap. Touching my glass in a pledge of new-found friendship, he asked if I would care to see something *Très interessant.* I nodded and followed him to the far end of the dining room where, mounted on the wall, he proudly displayed a framed photograph of a Merchant Marine crew holding a Life Preserver bearing the name of an American Tanker torpedoed a few miles south of Jacmel. The survivors were guests of the Excelsior for several weeks before returning to the United States.

Then, with the sly smile of a stage Magician about to perform an astounding trick, he led me to the opposite wall of the dining room and another framed photograph. Posing in front of the Excelsior were other war-time guests of Jacmel's finest and only hotel. Backs straight, smiling triumphantly at the camera, their white tropical uniforms immaculate, I saw the crew of the German U-Boat that sank the American tanker. *Le Propriétaire* explained that in 1942 German submarines prowling the waters south of Jacmel, unable to resist the lure of his fine French cuisine, dined at the Excelsior several times. They were charming guests and next morning, before dawn, they returned to sea to resume their deadly mission.

Ti Jean was a handsome twelve year old Bondservant serving as the hotel's waiter, bus boy, and porter. I guessed his age to be eight or nine, his normal growth stunted by years of starvation. *Le Propriétaire* explained he was one of many Marbial valley's children whose only hope of survival was in cities where they were sold by desperate parents unable to feed their families. At eighteen, when their Bond-contract expired, they usually remained at their jobs as paid employees if not replaced by unpaid Bondservants. My Host ignored this resemblance to slavery by challenging my discomfiting questions.

"Don't you think servitude is much better than seeing children with swollen bellies swallow dirt to stifle their hunger pangs?" he asked. I nodded, agreeing I had much to learn about such extreme poverty. And so once again I was witness to a world divided between rich and poor, powerful and powerless, privileged and humiliated without any possibility of change. Perhaps Max Seligman was right. Fighting for the dignity and sanctity of every human life is like "pissing in the wind." A futile task for Idealists.

Next morning, at sunrise, awakened by a triumphant Rooster crowing under my window, a cup of hot Haitian coffee at my bedside, I recalled Robert Louis Stevenson's statement - "Every day is a fresh beginning. Every morn the world is born anew." Looking out at the Caribbean, as the rising sun slowly abandoned for a day the black hole beyond the horizon where it rested all night, I experienced the innocent happiness of a child who believes everything is possible. Forgotten for a moment were Haiti's intractable problems of poverty, backwardness, starvation and human bondage that seemed at this moment diminished by early morning laughter and song as Jacmel, like a sparkling jewel set beside a silver sea slowly came to life.

Abelard Dessenclos, an Agronomist from the United Nation's Food and Agriculture Organization, arrived at the Excelsior in an ancient pick-up truck to drive me to the UN's Marbial Valley Compound several miles north of Jacmel. Handsome, with the detached appearance of a thoughtful Academic more comfortable in a Lecture Hall than in a rural impoverished valley, he drove with impressive skill avoiding the road's deepest pot holes and ruts.

Born and raised in Haiti, Abelard Dessenclos graduated Cornell University's School of Agriculture returning to his homeland to teach rural Haitians how to feed their families on rehabilitated farmland. Like other Elite Haitians participating in the UN's Technical Assistance Project, he was an exception to a rigid Caste system where French-speaking, cultured, light-skinned Haitians usually cared nothing about the fate of Creole-speaking, uneducated black Peasants living and dying unseen and without hope.

Abelard, like other Haitian Instructors I met at the UN Compound had seeing eyes and a feeling heart and his devotion to his less fortunate countrymen was inspiring. "Starvation in Haiti comes from ignorance of conservation or fertilization methods," Abelard Dessenclos explained. "Our once productive land is worn out. Every available acre is farmed by successive generations struggling to grow more from less and less productive land." He continued talking as we followed a shallow mud-colored river into the valley. "Planting the same crop year after year reduces yields below what hard-working families need to feed themselves."

Pausing to expand his thoughts he turned and nodded, his eyes a flashing intensity. "Starvation in Haiti is Man-made," Abelard Dessenclos insisted, tightening his grip on the steering wheel as we hit another bump in the road. "And Haiti can eliminate famine in less than a generation," he continued, "with no more than a little basic education." Then, turning his head away as if embarrassed by this display of unrestrained emotion, he fell silent concentrating his attention on the road ahead. For several miles his reluctance to speak persisted and I sensed something awkward distancing us from each other.

I thought perhaps he saw me as another white American burdened by all the cruel racial prejudices of the 1950's. Trying to correct Abelard's unwarranted assumption, to somehow regain some personal contact, I told him my brother was class of 1942 at Cornell, a friend of Brud Holland, the University's Black All-American football star. He replied with a disinterested nod. Didn't much follow football, he said. Soccer was his game. After another mile of uncomfortable silence, hoping to break through his cool reserve I tried again. "How did you like Ithaca?" I asked. "Cold. Very cold," he said, and all I could think about was how awkward human encounters become when complicated by the question of race. Obviously living in the United States was not an experience an intelligent, cultured and Elite Haitian wanted to talk about. Not after residing for several years in Paris where his human dignity was respected in a beautiful city where the tyranny of skin color did not rule.

"I count it little being barred from those who undervalue me," wrote Poet Langston Hughes fleeing to France to raise children undamaged by racial bigotry. "I have my own soul's ecstasy," Langston Hughes insisted, writing: "No man, my son, can batter down the far-flung ramparts of the mind." True. True, I thought, thinking about the man seated beside me retreating into his fortress of well-educated dignity.

Passing a small village near the UN Compound, a cluster of white-washed shacks, the road forded the river we followed from Jacmel. Abelard Dessanclos stopped in the middle of the shallow stream and pointed to the women washing clothes, gossiping, and bathing themselves and their children in the muddy water.

"There's the problem," he said. "that must be changed. Our people use that filthy sewer for everything. They wash clothes, bathe and drink the water animals pollute."

I saw an ancient tableau. A dozen women and children, some naked. Innocent beauty. Biblical. Without anticipating the impact of my words I commented: "The pencil of God has no eraser."

Dessanclos turned and stared at me astonished. Then laughing a full and joyous laugh he poked his finger into my arm. "You have read the Marcelin brothers?"

"Yes," I said. "*The Pencil of God* and *Canape Vert.* They won the Prix de Goncourt last year."

"How about Jacques Roumain's *Masters of the Dew?*" he asked.

"No. Haven't read that book"

"Well read Jacques Roumain and you will understand Haiti."

So that's how our friendship began. Two citizens of The Republic of Letters driving along a miserable rural road in Haiti's Marbial Valley discussing French Literature. What the African Poet Senghor called sharing "the Civilization of the Universal". We held a college Bull session on wheels bouncing over pot holes and ruts on our way to understanding each other and the world we live in.

Abelard was hungry to talk. He missed cosmopolitan Port Au Prince. Living and working isolated among peasants combined his great sense of *Noblesse Oblige* with intellectual boredom. He welcomed my visit.

On my last night in Port Au Prince before travelling to Jacmel, Antoine Bervan, a Haitian Diplomat and friend of a college classmate, during a gracious gourmet dinner explained although Haitians dance and sing to African rhythms their minds are dressed in French clothing. They also maintain a closeness to nature and a strong bond with ancestors unknown to Europeans.

Which led me to consider the clothes my mind wears. I like to think myself liberal, tolerant, without prejudice about race or color. But here in a remote Haitian valley, as the only white in a sea of négritude I didn't feel conspicuous as much as I sensed my humanity being tested. To be seen as another prejudiced white would preclude all possibility of winning the confidence of the Haitians I hoped to understand and write about.

Although the Marbial Valley in no way resembled Harlem's 125th street, both places contradicted conventional white knowledge about racial tensions. In 1941, ignoring warnings about being mugged, I went to hear Louis Armstrong at Harlem's Apollo theater with a friend who was an accomplished Jazz pianist. We were two white teen-agers in an all-black audience caught up in Armstrong's music without feeling threatened. So ignoring frightening newspaper reports we discovered all Blacks do not regard all whites as oppressors or think of themselves as victims. And so, after a few days in the Marbial Valley I learned that despite 19 years of occupation by United States Marines, who were predominantly prejudiced

Southerners, Haitians do not view all white Americans as incorrigibly racist, cruel and unjust.

I found I was regarded as just another human being who evoked laughter when I tried to speak Creole and looked ridiculous riding around on a small, emaciated mule. I was neither a white nor a *Gen de couleur.* I was only *L'Écrivain.* The writer.

Emanuel Gabriel Francois added another dimension to my understanding of the tyranny of skin color. A graduate of Columbia University's Teachers College, author of a Creole language text book, Headmaster of the UN school and Project Director, Professor Francois was handsome, black, and qualified to be a member of Haiti's Elite by intellect and the content of his character rather than the color of his skin. Devoted to teaching Peasants to read and write Creole, he defied the power of the Church and the Elite political leadership who dressed their minds in European clothing insisting all education be taught in French. Like Abelard Dessanclos he was a traitor to his class. An Elitist who believed the UN's attempt to eliminate illiteracy was only possible for as long as Paul Magloire, the first black President in sixteen years remained in office. He saw the coming year as a window of opportunity. Haiti's future would hopefully be determined by more than a tragic past.

The most imposing building in the UN Compound was a one-room schoolhouse open on all sides shielded from the sun and rain by an enormous tin roof sheltering more than one hundred students. The girls in spotless white blouses or knee-length pinafores. The boys in short-sleeved white shirts and blue shorts assembled in front of the school as Professor Francois explained the purpose of my visit. Well-fed, smiling, they politely repressed laughter as I greeted them with my primitive Creole. Absent were the spindly legs and swollen malnutrition bellies I saw on my tortured journey to Jacmel. They were healthy, literate children with a future, and if Emanuel Gabrielle Francois was their Pied Piper leading them towards a promising tomorrow, the instrument he was using was Haiti's maternal language. Creole.

Also at Marbial, two World Health Organization specialists in Tropical Medicine combated Yaws, Hookworm, Malaria, Yellow Fever, and other debilitating intestinal infections that caused the dispirited lethargy of many adults. What the Elite called lazy, shiftless Peasants without ambition were in fact men and women suffering from chronic illness that could be alleviated with Penicillin. Dr. Leon Bingham, a US Public Health Service doctor from New Orleans, and Dr. Dallaire from Algeria, toured the valley to inject the sick with hypodermic needles and were affectionately known as "The Two Pricks". But no antibiotic could eliminate re-infection from Hookworm in barefooted Peasants forever walking on toxic soil.

Henri Martineaux who taught carpentry and rope-making from Sisal fibers, or finding wells or springs of drinkable water, was my escort, translator, and eloquent guide to the mysteries of rural Haiti. Growing up in an Elite culture that looked down on anyone working with their hands, he nevertheless labored *comme un cheval* to give his people what they needed to escape unbearable poverty. Weighing near three hundred pounds, his volcanic energy and enthusiasm seemed truly *un force de nature*. An exhausting day with Martineaux under a blazing tropical sun tested my determination to see everything he insisted on showing me.

I could hardly wait for sunset when the entire UN Staff assembled at Madame Durand's table to enjoy one of her exquisite dinners in the cool of the evening. Madame Durand, daughter of a former Haitian Supreme Court Justice, managed the several Cays or one-room cottages, adjacent to a dining Pavillon where hours of brilliant conversation accompanied our meals. As I listened to the Staff talk I felt both ignorant and enthralled by passionate disputes about poetry, philosophy and the latest cultural news from Paris. Everyone at the table participated intellectually in a world foreign to me and, as I struggled to understand their classic Parisian French, I was again reminded of the absurdity of employing complexion as a criterion of human value. Accepted and valued when in France as superior human beings, these Haitians were critical of their humiliating experiences in the United States. I made no attempt to defend the indefensible and mentioned the prejudice expressed by *Le Propriétaire* in Jacmel. "Prejudice," Madame Durand replied, "provides the last line of defense for the status quo. Keeping things as they are, insisting it is futile to educate Peasants maintains the aristocrats' monopoly on jobs and wealth. Upper class Haitians bitterly oppose our effort to improve the well-being of *Les Noirs*. The Blacks. They fear a social revolution."

Armed with nothing more potent than a Creole textbook, a hypodermic needle, a shovel and a hoe, these idealistic revolutionaries, financed by the United Nations, were addressing the intractable problems of their homeland with intelligence and passion. They worked without assurance their project would

31

eliminate illiteracy and starvation in the Marbial, and then expand to other regions. But they did hope the skills they taught in this impoverished valley would someday become a permanent part of Public Education in Haiti. A very high hope indeed.

Reading Haitian history however was not encouraging. During the occupation American authorities were accused of establishing a rival educational system. In 1934, when the Marines withdrew, their plans to improve education were dismissed as a foreign intrusion into Haitian life. Training teachers willing to live a hard life in rural isolation among illiterate Peasants was as daunting an obstacle to overcome as the political and social implications of mass education in Creole. A language without schoolbooks, literature, or established spelling before the arrival of the United Nations. Underdeveloped, plagued with the problems of a Third World country, predominately rural Haiti was roadless, with few industries or urban centers to provide jobs in tourism or manufacturing. Migration or exile deprived Haiti of educated professionals who rebuild their lives and careers abroad and rarely return to their homeland. Abelard Dessanclos and Professor Francois were exceptions, educated abroad and now working to change Haiti's future, they were hopeful about the UN project's fate. "History does not have to repeat itself," they insisted, referring to the failed reforms of the American occupation. Within ten years the improved infrastructure acquired during 19 years of assistance; the new roads, schools, and clinics crumbled and soon were abandoned. Haiti became what it is today. A human and political disaster. Unable to feed itself.

Looking back more than 58 years I realize I witnessed the first test of the question: "Can any Technical Assistance or Foreign Aid Program succeed without transforming the social and economic culture of a country?" A crucial question being tested today.

My most informative introduction to the real Haiti, the eternal Haiti, the intractable culture so resistant to change, occurred on the back of a small spindly-legged mule following Henri Martineaux riding a slightly larger animal. For five hours he led me along a narrow mountain trail alternately traversing and then descending steep hillsides in a tortured bone-jarring journey to one of Marbial's distant *Tonnelles,* an open-sided Palm thatched shed where we were to attend a wedding. On slopes so steep I could reach up and touch the ground, my sure-footed mule humped and swayed sending shock waves up my spine with each heavy step. No doubt we were a comic sight. Looking like an overweight Don Quixote, Henri Martineaux's enormous bulk overflowed his saddle as I, feeling myself a loyal Sancho Panza twisted and turned on my wheezing mount to ease the pain of each unforgiving blow to my rear. Our mules miraculously never stumbled as we jogged along the precipitous path without speaking.

On my mind was last night's dinner where Professor Francois, after a second glass of rum, insisted the Marcellin brothers created a truer portrait of Haiti than could be found in Jacques Roumain's *Masters of The Dew.* Abelard Dessanclos passionately disagreed and I was a fascinated witness to a polite literary brawl. A heated discussion I struggled to understand.

"Haitians are not, and will never be a rural proletariat," Emanuel Gabriel Francois said. "Haitians, like most uneducated Peasants live in their imaginations in a world of ever-present beliefs. Or myths. Their world is our Elite world turned upside down. Haitian peasants do not always see what we see. What is immediate and real for us is for them something above and beyond what educated people call reality." He concluded by saying "most Haitians blame everything bad in their lives as coming from the displeasure of their Gods."

When we stopped to rest our backsides and our mules, I asked Henri Martineaux what he thought of last night's argument. He laughed explaining that's the way town intellectuals talk when they flee the sophisticated world of the cities to return to the people. "Such abstract discussions do little for the lives of the poor *Ti-nègres*," he said. "President Paul Magloire made few speeches. He came to the Marbial valley and built a concrete three foot high Butcher's Block so pigs and chickens could be slaughtered and butchered off the ground. Actions not words are what Haiti needs. Dig a well. A latrine. An irrigation ditch. Or terrace a slope to hold the soil. Leave the talk to the Haitians who write books. Did you know our Bibliotheque National has more than five thousand books written by our intellectuals and still our people are starving?"

Arriving at our destination, a *La Tonnelle* erected in the center of a small village, Henri Martineaux was greeted with great respect and honor. Under this large palm-thatched shed the women of the hamlet dressed in ankle length spotless white dresses and wearing large wide-brimmed hats served coffee to the guests.

Nearby, sipping something stronger than coffee a Ra Ra band of drummers, musicians travelling from village to village to accompany Saturday night dancing, awaited the festivities.

Henri Martineaux explained the exceptional significance of a formal wedding ceremony where *Plaçage*, unmarried common-law relationships, a custom imposed by slavery to benefit slave owners, is almost universal. A *Prêtre Savan*, an unordained Bush Priest presides with a blend of Catholic and Voudon rituals that satisfy all aspects of the Peasants faith in a supreme being.

Women pray for fertility at statues of the Virgin Mary also called Grand Ezile, the black Venus or Goddess of Love and St. Patrick, who drove the snakes from Ireland is also Damballa Ouedo, the African snake God, Master of Heaven. Belief in the power of one God does not preclude faith in other Gods. In their ancient wisdom *Les nègres* enjoy the protection of both religions.

The proud wedding party arrived on foot, the bride wearing a white full-length dress beside the groom in a double-breasted linen suit, white shirt and bow tie. The family in dazzling white suits and dresses were led by a father wearing an eye-catching bright red necktie. A truly royal procession.

A family display of honor and dignity like that of Kings. A rainbow of happiness in black and white and red. "Give me a rainbow, you who have given us the rain" are the lyrics of a truly poignant song. And this family was that rainbow in living Technicolor.

And what of the bride and groom, I wondered? How aware are they of rising in Haiti's rigid caste system by rejecting *Plaçage*? A cohabitation most

Haitian's accept as respectable? Can the honor, dignity and enhanced self-respect of sanctified marriage somehow mitigate the socially destructive consequences of centuries of white-on-black humiliation? Does Holy Matrimony celebrated by an unordained Bush Priest vanquish a cultural habit imposed by slavery?

What Sociologists call Upward Mobility is rare in Haiti. Each generation of *Les nègres* rarely rise above their parents' destiny. Sacramental marriages, however, unlike learning French are more than an effort to move up socially and professionally but rather are a statement like chanting "I am a Man! I am a Man!" by Civil Rights marchers in the streets of Alabama. In 1951, in Haiti, a legally sanctified peasant marriage is a precursor of change. Touching the future with a promise to love, honor and obey.

The next morning, after a night of dancing energized by Taffin, raw Haitian Rum, Henri Martineaux led our return to Marbial. Continuing last evenings festive mood he began singing "Pata Mama Tombe" a sorrowful Creole lament that is also somehow light-hearted. Courageous. Henri translated into French: "Mon Pere and Ma Mère sont Tombe", "My mother and Father are dead" rendered in sing-song Creole as "Pata Mama Tombe." And so began another Creole lesson: "Je suis malade" in French, "I am sick" became in Creole "Moins malade." "Me sick." A short, clear statement without a verb.

After joining Henri singing several verses about an orphan boy who happily accepts life with no possessions but a mule and endless drudgery I began to yodel. Overcome with laughter Martineaux nearly fell off his mule. He then insisted I teach him the trick of sliding back and forth from a whole note to a falsetto. A skill I acquired imitating Sepp Rusch, an Austrian ski instructor at Vermont's Mount Mansfield. Martineaux was particularly fond of a Swiss "Cuckoo Clock" song insisting I repeat it several times. Somehow, gentled by laughter and yodeling our return trip was less agonizing.

Dinner at Madame Durand's table that evening was most welcome although a constant shifting in my seat made the painful condition of my saddle-sore bottom a subject of amused comment. And again another well-mannered political brawl accompanied our meal. A heated argument about the 1915-1934 occupation described the mixed blessing of well-meaning American intervention. The roads, bridges, schools and hospitals left behind soon deteriorated. What remained; a memory of Mississippi-style racism supporting the privileged position of the light-skinned Elite who were maintained in office by prejudiced American authorities who believed blacks were incapable of governing.

The racial and cultural barriers to economic progress persisted during decades of corruption under black politicians who replaced the Elites in 1934. As one corrupt and repressive regime succeeded another, Haiti's expanding population struggled to survive on a shrinking food supply.

Emanuel Gabriel Francois spoke of the future. "When we leave what happens afterwards is the question. After so many cruel foreign interventions Haiti remains unchanged. No matter how successful we are at Marbial what Haitians and their government do for themselves when we are gone will be decisive."

In 1918, during the occupation, President Wilson's under secretary of the Navy, Franklin Delano Roosevelt drafted the Haitian Constitution. In October 1934, as President, he announced the American withdrawal in a charming speech in French stating: "When I die, I think Haiti is going to be written on my heart because for all these years I have had the most intense interest in the Republic of Haiti and the development of its people in a way that will never mean exploitation by any other nation."

Eloquent words, said Henri Martineaux, do little for the lives of the *Ti-nègres.* Actions not words are what Haiti needs. Dig a well. A latrine. An irrigation ditch. Fine words are for books in the National Library in Port Au Prince.

And so, sadly, with the demise of Paul Magloire's Presidency, the UN's Technical Assistance Program terminated with a shift of power to the Elite. Once again Haiti's intractable caste system overwhelmed all efforts to bring about social and economic change. Then, for thirty years, the Duvalier dictatorship empowered by Ton Ton Macoute Death Squads ravaged an already desolate nation. The next fifteen years of coups by Masters of Misery, corrupt Politicians and Generals, destroyed all hope for a better life. Today, desperate Haitians risk their lives at sea in decrepit sailboats rather than remain and starve in their impoverished homeland.

Sergeant Poisson's painting, presented to me the day I left Haiti and now on my wall, depicts a young girl gazing out her bedroom window down an empty road leading to a solitary Palm tree. Whatever may or may not come of her romantic dreams of the future, I am certain that in the Marbial valley survives, despite

58 years of callous indifference, a three-foot high concrete Butcher's Block where Haitian mothers once came to beg food for their starving children.

A legacy, they say, paid for not from the National Treasury, but from President Magloire's own pocket.

BEIJING

1966. During Chairman Mao's Cultural Revolution, instigated by his Little Red Book of instructions for fanatical students, Mao's teachings resulted in the wanton destruction of China's historic cultural and educational heritage. "Abolish all rules and disciplines, especially foreign ways of thinking which limit the mind," Chairman Mao wrote. "The more science you learn - the less revolutionary you become," he proclaimed. "It is better to be a 'Red Guard' than be an Expert" responded students waving Mao's book while burning schools and Universities, humiliating and often beating their teachers to death.

Chairman Mao encouraged mindless violence. "When one is a Revolutionary one does not need to study in a University," he commented. "We must not cultivate Bookworms" became the prevalent mantra of that destructive decade.

After ten years without functioning schools and Universities encouraging students to destroy old customs, old habits, old culture and old thinking, this madness subsided. Brutalized Educators and Intellectuals banished to years of re-education planting and harvesting rice, were again recognized as vital to China's ability to become part of a globally integrated world economy.

But only a few desperately needed teachers survived the Cultural Revolution, and by 1980, nearly a quarter of a million Chinese students went overseas seeking an education. Of those lucky or connected enough to get visas to study abroad, fewer than one in five returned.

In 1985, after several years as a Satellite Broadcasting Pioneer, I became involved with another promising new technology, writing and producing Interactive Educational Programs. A visual, emotional, and intellectual learning experience made possible by combining a computer and a videodisc. By touching the monitor's screen students obtain what they need to know, at their own pace, following individualized pathways. Learning from their mistakes, students make right or wrong choices with the consequences of each wrong choice demonstrated and corrected. The mental process of gathering and analyzing information, thinking - as well as solid factual information is taught.

A 30 minute interactive videodisc using still photos, motion pictures, computer graphics and animation can convey as much as three hours of information and learning. "Build a better mousetrap and the world will beat a path to your door" is a saying attributed to Henry Ford, Thomas Edison, Alexander Graham Bell and several other anonymous founders of modern industry. Interactive Discovery Learning with computers and videodiscs was a vast improvement over conventional teaching methods. Definitely a better mousetrap.

A phone call from the State Department confirmed this. A delegation led by Wang Jizi of Beijing's Stone Group Computers were guests of our government's Technical Exchange Program, here to learn about American technology with a particular interest in interactive videodisc teaching.

"Would I be willing to demonstrate my latest programs including your proposed College Preparatory Curriculum?" he asked.

"When will they be in New York?" I replied.

"Next week."

"How many in the Delegation?"

"Ten."

"All right," I said. "Next Tuesday at my office from ten AM to one PM and the State Department pays for lunch."

"Thank you very much," he said, appreciating my reply. He then explained that this nationwide Tour had embarrassed our government. Most prominent Computer Companies refused to expose their latest technology to a country violating all International copyright laws with impunity. Closed doors, they insisted, should be the consequences of China's flagrant piracy. And my door was open. I sensed an opportunity. And certainly there was nothing secret about interactive technology. All that was needed was the right hardware and the brains to program it.

The demonstration was a success. The Delegation recognized that interactive training met China's need to raise students to more advanced standards bringing them a wealth of scientific and technical learning. A Core Curriculum of Chemistry, Physics, Mathematics, and Computer Science certainly are essential foundations of economic development in all nations regardless of political ideology.

I quoted my Dartmouth College Professor Louis Benezet's remark "to save the world save one student at a time," adding my conviction that the essential prelude to exceptional achievement is to challenge and pressure students, evoking a sense of high purpose combining outstanding intellectual ability with character, motivation and idealistic intent.

Wang Jizhi nodded. "Yes," he replied. "China is most concerned with the quality as well as the quantity of Middle School and University students.

Our sober two hour lunch confirmed that in contrast to Russians the Chinese would rather eat than drink. And twelve months passed before I heard from any member of the Delegation again. Friends experienced with doing business in China advised me not to expect anything to result from the demonstration. The Chinese meet, talk, correspond and in the end do nothing. Investing money and time in them is too often futile.

Then, several months after the Tiananmen Square debacle I received a FAX from Wang Jizhi of Beijing's Stone Group, China's largest Computer Company. "I take great pleasure to invite you to come to Beijing and visit our Company during the week of September 10th to discuss development of our Interactive College Preparatory Curriculum. I trust we will make a satisfying decision and go further in our collaboration in this field."

An invitation I could not refuse.

My Brooklyn neighborhood, East 28th and East 29th street between Kings Highway and Quentin Road had several highly celebrated "Boys on the Block". Sidney Franklin, a Jewish American, became one of Mexico's celebrated Toreadors drawing enormous crowds attracted as much by his unique heritage as by his skill fighting Bulls. And following the attack on Pearl Harbor, America's first publicized Heroes were East 29th street's Meyer Levin and his Pilot Colin Kelly killed while supposedly sinking the Japanese Battleship Haruna. That the Haruna survived their attack was ignored in our desperate need for Heroes provided by Levin, one of our more famous "Boys on the Block".

In 1979, while browsing in a Bookstore I was surprised to discover a book written by another one of our remarkable "Boys on the Block". Sidney Shapiro's *An American in China* relates his story of thirty years in the People's Republic by an American who remained after the Nationalist government fled to Taiwan. "China from within" attracted many interested readers.

Although the Shapiro family lived across the street from my home for twelve years, and Sidney's mother was a close and supportive friend of my mother during her long illness, I vaguely remembered Sidney. The last I heard of him before his disappearance was that he was a Lawyer like his father and writing for the theatrical newspaper "Variety".

I continued reading the book jacket describing how in 1947 Sidney, a young American ex-GI, learning Chinese in the Army, and now a Lawyer, sailed for China driven by wanderlust and a fascination for the Orient. He arrived in Shanghai in the midst of a savage Civil War in a nation undergoing a radical political transformation.

Sidney stayed, married, and became a Chinese citizen working as a Translator as well as an author of books on the Chinese legal system and the history of the Jews in China.

Then in 1984, I read an article about Sidney headlined: "Big Bagel Baker Bares History of Jews in China." The review of his book quoted him as saying: "I never stopped being Jewish in the cultural sense, with my fondness for Jewish food and Jewish humor." And so Sidney began baking Bagels, his home becoming a mandatory tourist stop for Jews visiting Beijing.

In 1990, after receiving Wang Jizhi's invitation I called the New American Library, Sidney's publisher, and obtained his FAX and telephone numbers.

Signing myself "one of the Boys on the Block" I sent a FAX announcing my September arrival and exploiting his declared love of Jewish humor asked if I could visit him and enjoy one of his Sesame Seed Bagels with cream cheese.

He immediately replied "welcome" requesting a favor. Would I go to Zabars on Broadway and 81st street and bring some Chocolate covered or Marble Halavah? It seems in all of China Halvah, his favorite delicacy, was unobtainable.

And so, en-route to Kennedy Airport I detoured to Manhattan and filled the empty spaces of my luggage with packages of Zabar's Internationally famous Halavah hoping the unheated luggage compartment of a 747 would prevent the Halavah from melting all over my clothes.

Wang Jizhi met me at Beijing airport with a car and driver and a University student to act as translator. He suggested I relax after my flight and see Beijing before beginning my arduous schedule of demonstrations. The Forbidden City, the Summer Palace, and Beijing's University comprised my tour of an ancient city being transformed into a modern Capitol. New Hotels, Skyscrapers, and wide avenues replaced the China of my imagination; old one and two storey wooden homes and buildings with tile roofs and carved window frames and doors were being demolished wherever I looked. In the narrow crowded streets of the old neighborhoods, freight carrying bicycles struggled through swarms of pedestrians who casually stepped aside like the parting of a human sea to enable cars to drive through. Cooking and heating with charcoal produced a blue haze mixed with a sulfur-sweet odor and the familiar smell of roasting chestnuts and fresh fruits and vegetables sold by street vendors.

Yes. Here was the China I expected. Unchanged. Exploding with humanity. Alive and well. And when from the wall above one of the Old Gates of the City, I saw in the distance rising columns of black smoke from coal-burning Steel Mills creating a dense layer of smog, it was apparent no nation escapes the price of progress bringing illness and death to millions.

Wang Jizhi carefully prepared for my visit. Working with the office of Li Tieying Chairman of the State Education Commission, Wang set up a demonstration for Teachers from Beijing's prestigious August First Middle School where hopefully 400 students would participate in a two year feasibility or Pilot study of our College Preparatory Curriculum. If valid educational test data confirmed the program's effectiveness, then 19 other Middle Schools would participate. We were demonstrating a program that seeks, finds and

47

nurtures promising students who would otherwise be lost in China's traditional educational process. One still dominated by the teachings of Confucius.

Wang Jizhi explained that it would help our audience understand our program if I wrote a brief introduction which he would translate and display on a Wall Poster or Banner in both English and Chinese. With apologies to Robert Frost I wrote:

"We are teachers
We bring lightning down from the sky
Into the growing minds of our future.
Fear not to use this powerful new educational tool
For it has been given to us by technology
And a history that embraces both Socrates and Confucius!"

The audience was enthralled. When operating the touch screen monitors they were like children with a new toy. The usual and anticipated resistance so prevalent in the United States to bringing Learning Machines into classrooms was not evident. Here was a remarkable educational Aid that truly assisted rather than threatened teacher's jobs.

That evening I called Sidney and he asked that I bring my driver to the phone for directions to 33 Nanguanfang, West City where I was expected for dinner. Driving through a labyrinth of alleys, lanes, and streets just wide enough for a small car, I drove by a familiar sight in Beijing's old neighborhoods. Seated on a chair in front of her home an Old Auntie, an elderly woman watched my car stop a few yards from

Sidney's gate. Ringing the bell I turned and smiled at her. She raised a hand to greet me and smiled, a more hospitable version of the Key Wardens supervising each floor of Moscow's Hotels.

After a warm reception I asked and Sidney explained that the Old Aunties were a holdover from the good old days, watching for unusual activities in their neighborhood, and since it was normal for the Shapiros to receive foreign visitors, the old lady would have nothing unusual to report. And what's more when the Old Aunties die out they are not replaced. An anachronism from the Civil War when all foreigners were suspected Foreign Devils.

Before 1949 and the flight of the Nationalist Government of Chiang Kai Shek to Taiwan, Sidney's home belonged to a wealthy merchant whose fate we never discussed. A spacious private Compound enclosed inside a high brick wall contained two houses. A small Cottage in the rear that previously housed servants, was now occupied by Sidney's daughter and son-in-Law both Doctors, and his granddaughter, a Middle School student. The larger house with a red tile roof vaguely resembled East 28th street, and as I walked from the gate to the front door I noticed several tons of coal piled up against one wall of the Compound. Heating and cooking fuel for the coming winter.

The Spartan-like interior was comfortable displaying attractive Chinese artifacts, several paintings, and a prominent photograph of Chou en-Lai, the Chinese Communist Leader most sympathetic to, and therefore most popular with our government. Called "Joe", and highly praised and publicized by Journalists, he was considered a friend during our war with Japan when "the Red Armies did most of the fighting against the Japs" while corrupt Nationalist Generals avoided battle and became wealthy selling weapons provided by our Lend-Lease program. The anti-Western paranoia of Chairman Mao ended our brief war-time cooperation with Communist China as the Cold War evolved into a fifty year conflict between Good and Evil.

Sidney's wife Phoenix entered the room and, as she held out her hand, I understood why Sidney never returned in 1947. Her grace and beauty were unique. A former actress, drama critic, and book editor, she moved and smiled with animated eyes expressing a succession of feelings that made dialogue unnecessary.

Dinner was more than a Sesame Seed Bagel. And, at the end of a sumptuous meal Sidney opened a precious package of chocolate covered Halavah as desert as we made plans for the days I was free of government meetings.

My meeting with Hu Zhao Guang President of Beijing's Special Economic Zone seemed to have as its main purpose an opportunity to host a mid-day banquet that continued until late afternoon. Seated at a large round table were more than twenty of his Staff to answer questions and help the President explain that Special Economic Zones encourage foreign investments by establishing free and open markets where, despite Marx and Lenin, making as much money as possible was the principal ideology. Stone Group Computers, with Capital provided by Mitsui of Japan was but one of many profitable corporations creating a new China.

As a guest at Wang Jizhi's home that evening, I learned more about what was happening in this new China. I asked about when the Communist take-over attracted so many foreigners with its promise of self-reliance, Proletarian values, and fulfillment of Socialist dreams. One of the guests laughed at my question. No doubt considering me naive. Blind to the reality around me. As if talking to a child he explained: "These old Leftists, Americans, Canadians, English, will be with us until they die clinging to political beliefs that most educated Chinese abandoned years ago. With more and more Socialist ideas discarded each year, their belief that their worn out ideology will somehow prevail is quite touching. Quixotic. Like The Man From La Mancha. Do you know that play?"

"Yes," I said. "My favorite song. The Impossible Dream."

Another guest, who had been playing the piano turned and said: "That's right. Impossible. Wrong-headed. You can't re-mold human nature to be something it is not."

A young woman, a Computer Programmer, interrupted. "You can't deny it worked for a while. There was very little theft. There was great community spirit. There was a common goal. That's all gone now except for the memory."

The next morning I drove with Sidney and Phoenix to the Great Wall and the Ming Tombs located several hours North of Beijing. With the vivid memory of childhood automobile trips dominated by an Uncle's Left-Wing political fervor, I determined to never discuss politics with Sidney. It was apparent

51

they had not been on an excursion for some time behaving like excited teen-agers, holding hands and enthusiastically pointing out sights of historic interest. They were my Tour Guides who love everything passing by our car. It was also apparent that after more than forty years they were still "in love" and unrestrained in showing their affection for each other. Slowly, without being asked, the story of their not always tranquil marriage emerged. For several years during the Cultural Revolution, Phoenix was sent out into the countryside for re-education planting and harvesting rice while Sidney, as a "Foreign Devil" experienced a limited kind of House Arrest.

Despite the suffering of all intellectuals in the 1960's and 1970's, and the death of more than 30 million Chinese in the great famines of 1960 to 1962, and the gradual abandonment of Socialist ideology in the 1980's, Sidney and Phoenix's enthusiasm for living in China seemed undiminished. I could only wonder, why? How was this possible after all they suffered?

At a leisurely, relaxed lunch that day I began to see what I had not seen before. They were happy here. Truly content. China was their spiritual home. The laid-back contemplative life style of China's ancient culture more than any political ideology held them enthralled.

I recalled reading an interview Sidney gave on one of his trips to the United States denying he was a Communist but stating: "I do heartily approve of what the Communists have done since 1949. They are creating a new interpretation of how to run a Socialist country."

Our famous American Playwright Arthur Miller, another "Brooklyn Boy" who was not from our "Block", in Beijing to direct "The Crucible" dramatizing our Salem Witch Trials, after visiting Sidney reported: "He persists in his warm and loving bondage to the sublime. The very same condition from which the Chinese are cautiously emerging." Miller then marveled at the "windless space Sidney seems to occupy where in truth nothing has penetrated in fifty years."

Was Sidney a political Rip Van Winkle? Morally blind to the lessons of History? A man disconnected from the struggle, unable to draw a line beyond which the State can not reach into an individual's life, accepting a society where only the State has rights and powers, and the person, like all personal property, belongs only to the Collective?

Was Miller's description of Sidney fair?

During the Blacklist years, Arthur Miller's refusal to be intimidated into cooperating with the Un-American Activities Committee when so many prominent artists compromised themselves was an inspiring demonstration of moral courage. To insist on the personal integrity of the individual speaking Truth to Power when confronted by publicity-seeking Witch Hunters, was no small achievement.

A man's hopes, dreams and choices are his life. Arthur Miller never abdicated his independence as a writer and citizen. Never assented to the idea that government policy alone is sacred and that every other human value should be sacrificed to it. "Freedom from violence and falsehood," he wrote, "is not an impossible dream as long as men of honor do not by their silence give their consent and allow the State unrestrained power over all our lives."

Two lives. Arthur and Sidney. Two boys from Brooklyn. One an uncompromising champion of Human Rights. And Sidney? Certainly a man following his destiny. Living his dream, driven by his great love for Phoenix and an ancient culture.

For many years Sidney was a member of the prestigious Chinese People's Political Consultive Council -- Advisors who many believe merely rubber stamp government policies. They are all well-known intellectuals and professionals from many nations who travel the world as articulate spokesmen for a political system that is disappearing. Privileged, some say, even pampered, travelling at government expense, Sidney and other Foreign Friends of China continue to dream their impossible dream adhering to the poet Langston Hughes' lyrical lines:

"Hold fast to dreams, for when dreams die, life is a broken-winged bird that can not fly."

After a series of successful demonstrations arranged by Wang Jizhi I left China confident that we had won approval of our programs at the hands-on working level at the Ministry of Education. There was nothing to do but wait for a final decision by Chairman Li Tieying and his superiors.

As my more experienced business associates predicted I never heard from Wang Jizhi again. Inquiries to the Ministry of Education over the next several years never once received a "Yes", a "No", or a "Maybe".

A Lecturer at the Yale China Society explained that China is trying to become a globally integrated market economy without fostering the culture of critical thinking they need if they want to grow.

The Chinese government fears a loss of control if students learn how, instead of what to think. And my interactive education program teaches thinking rather than blind worship of authority. Until this generation of Leaders passes, my trip to China pursued another impossible dream.

And as for Sidney's life and career, I believe his most enduring achievement is a four volume translation of the 14th century classic "Outlaws of The Marsh". By sharing his passion for Chinese Culture, he enriched the lives of countless readers of great literature.

MOSCOW

Two distinct categories of travelers inhabit Westchester County. Constipated Commuters noted for early morning departures, and a few less harried self-employed who regularly ride to New York on mid-day trains. For twenty years my daily routine enabled me to escape abrasive Rush Hour agonies. After writing all morning at my Dobbs Ferry home the 1:10 to Grand Central provided time for a forty minute nap that became my only respite in a long hard working day. But not every day.

My neighbor Alan Schneider, after awakening at noon, often rushed to our train buoyant with recharged energy and an appetite for conversation. With ambivalent feelings I abandoned all hope of sleep as he sat beside me and tilted his ever-present baseball cap on the back of his head. Wearing canvas sneakers, of medium height, Alan's irrepressible enthusiasm made him seem taller as he talked, bounced, jiggled, and vibrated in his seat. For Alan getting to know you was a passion as enduring as Love. His insatiable curiosity nourished his ability to recreate the diverse characters he directed so realistically on stage. Alan was the most favored director of Samuel Beckett, Edward Albee, and Harold Pinter. *Waiting For Godot* and *Who's Afraid of Virginia Woolf* were but a few of his many triumphs resulting from boundless energy, strong feelings and deep theatrical perception.

As a friend and fellow Metro-North passenger Alan could not be ignored. The dramatic story of his life was told and retold several times from birth in Kharkov Russia to growing up in Baltimore followed by student days at Cornell where having drinks At Theodore Zinks was an intoxicated undergraduate ritual. Alan was a listener as well as an exuberant talker. He insisted on knowing everything about everyone. Marriages, divorces, and careers were exhumed with attention to specific detail that rejected all generalities. He relentlessly repeated questions until a completely candid reply broke through walls of personal privacy.

"Where the Hell are you going this time?" Alan asked pointing his thumb at my luggage on the rack above our seat. Alan's hands were as expressive as words carving silent figures of speech in the air as he talked. Words and action combined to clarify meaning. All existence was Theater. Alan was the brilliant Director and I was about to be given a walk-on part in play called Life.

"Moscow," I replied.

Alan became silent. Motionless. After a long pause he asked, "When are you leaving?"

"Tonight. 11 P.M."

For the next few miles Alan stared out the window and said nothing. I unfolded the Times and began to read about Watergate. As we entered the Tunnel into Grand Central Alan suddenly grabbed my arm.

In a quiet voice he said "There's something really important you can do for me in Moscow."

"What's that?" I asked, startled by his behavior.

"Do you have time for coffee?"

"Yes."

"It's a long story," he said. "And I don't believe there's a happy ending."

Over English muffins and three cups of coffee Alan explained what I could do for him in Moscow. His Russian cousin killed himself after expulsion from Medical School. Although an outstanding student and winner of many Academic Honors applying for an Exit Visa to Israel destroyed any possibility of a medical career. His parents, both well-known Doctors, were distraught, inconsolable, grieving as only Russian Jews can grieve. Alan was worried. His cousins had not responded to several letters or phone calls. He did not know whether they were alive or dead. Would I phone them? Find their apartment? Hand deliver another letter containing Visa Applications, Affidavits and other information encouraging them to come to the United States?

Without hesitation or thought I agreed. About 6 P.M. that evening, just before leaving for JFK, a Messenger Service Cyclist arrived at my East 51st street office with a thick envelope containing legal documents, letters and photographs. Alan would not be denied. My role, my walk-on part suddenly became real. Acquired wings. I would be flying to a sinister and daunting destination with unknown consequences for myself and his cousins.

I did not tell Alan what he certainly knew. Encouraging Russian citizens to go abroad as Tourists and then defect was probably futile and possibly dangerous.

As my Swiss Air Jumbo Jet climbed to cruising altitude I had several double whiskeys, lay down across a row of seats, covered myself with a blanket and slept all the way to Geneva. After refueling both the plane and passengers, the flight continued as from my window I watched an endless panorama of Eastern Europe pass under me. Extending to the far horizon, the undulating ocean of the Polish and Russian steppes were the Breadbasket fought over for centuries by Kings, Emperors and Dictators striving for Lebensraum for expanding populations. Two thousand miles of unpaved roads became quagmires of viscous mud in rain, and waist deep snow in winter defeating every attempt to conquer this land. Napoleon and Hitler lost vast armies. Panzer Divisions conquering Europe with Blitzkreigs, advancing a hundred miles a day on paved roads, were now stalled, compelled to wait for dirt roads to dry and harden. Hitler's Lightning War, moving and supplying three million soldiers over a distance greater than New York to Denver was more than an illusion. More than folly. It was hubris endorsed by ambitious Generals and an entire nation enthralled by their God-given destiny.

"Deutchland Uber Alles" wasted fifty million lives and looking out the window during the long flight to Moscow I appreciated more than ever the difference between a Hot and Cold War.

The International Arrivals Area at Moscow Airport seemed familiar. I had seen it before in numerous anti-Communist movies. Brutal Soldiers with automatic weapons guarded Exits. Grim-faced

Customs Inspectors checked luggage and Passports with no hint of hospitality. I felt I had entered the forbidding portals of a Police State and was unwelcome. Smiles and human friendliness were indeed casualties of the Cold War. All who entered Russia were presumed a threat reminding me of the Reception Hall at Sing Sing Prison where wives and friends of Inmates endured the hostility of intimidating Guards rummaging through hand bags and gift packages as if no visitor or citizen was ever innocent.

"I have seen the Future and it works," said apologists for Soviet terror visiting Russia. Blinded by Ideology, they saw only what confirmed their fanatic belief that a society operating like a prison could long endure.

Intourist, the government Travel Agency arranged my Visas, Hotel reservations, and a car and driver with a full schedule of business meetings that only allowed time in the evenings for the Ballet and Theater. I was not free to come and go on my own as the hovering presence of Boris, my grim-faced driver made evident. He introduced himself at the Passport Control desk and led me with my luggage to a familiar black Zim limousine, a copy of a 1946 American Packard. The silence of our wordless drive from the airport into Moscow was abruptly broken as we passed a War Memorial of rusted trucks and shattered Tanks. "Here," Boris explained as if reading to a child from a Guidebook, "At the very last Stop of the Trolley Line, on the outskirts of the city, the heroic people of Moscow came out and defeated the Fascists."

"Yes," I replied. "The beginning of the end of Hitler." Boris grunted. Satisfied with my comment.

He looked into the rear view mirror and studied me. It was bitter cold. I wore my heavy wool Navy Greatcoat with brass buttons replaced and the high collar turned up around my neck. I sank back in my seat and closed my eyes exhausted by my journey returning his silence with calculated indifference. I could tolerate his rudeness for a week. Ten days perhaps. He would be no more insulting than a Paris Taxi driver who hated tourists in general and Americans in particular.

Boris nodded and even smiled a little when I told him I did not need a car until noon tomorrow. Like other Intourist chauffeurs free of their assigned riders, Boris Moonlighted as a public Taxi, a fact I discovered and ignored when walking to my hotel one night seeing him solicit passengers outside the Bolshoi Theater. His little secret somehow diluted my paranoia about Boris. He was human after all. A clandestine Capitalist in business for himself despite the teachings of Karl Marx.

Every floor of the old National Hotel adjacent to Red Square was monitored by an unsmiling Concierge who controlled room keys. I handed her a receipt issued by the Desk Clerk in the lobby and, as she examined the document and confirmed that I had indeed paid for my room and was entitled to a key, I struggled to subdue my exasperation. Travelling twenty-four hours I wanted only to sleep and was in no mood for her bureaucratic hostility. In a language that vaguely resembled English the Concierge explained I was to return the key every morning before leaving the hotel. She stared at me from behind her desk, hesitating, withholding my room key until I acknowledged understanding her instructions. Then the key ungraciously dropped into my open and grateful hand.

The next day in Minister Chazov's office our meeting began at a Buffet Table overloaded with bowls of Caviar, bottles of Vodka, long loaves of Black bread and Blini. His Staff, privileged members of the Nomenclatura were in a party mood, joyfully eating and raising their glasses in respectful toasts to our future relationship. They were most interested in the idea of Satellite Broadcasting and working with my company, Overseas Satellite Programs. Ten years before CNN made world-wide Satellite news coverage commonplace, only World Cup Soccer, Muhammad Ali Fights, and the Pope's Christmas message used this technology. COMSAT, an International Consortium of eighty nations built and operated Earth Station Uplinks to their Satellite and encouraged the transmission of the type of Public Affairs programming I was producing.

After more drinks, and a blurred bi-lingual discussion of the responsibilities of a Participating Broadcaster who must conform to the technical procedures of other stations in the Satellite Network, someone questioned me about my old Navy Greatcoat.

Did you fight in the Great Patriotic War?" asked the Minister's Translator proudly wearing a row of Medals on his chest. When I replied I was a Navy pilot he raised his glass and toasted with unrestrained emotion - "Convoys!... Murmansk!...Studebaker trucks! Beautiful Sherman Tanks!" After brief applause and hilarious laughter followed by another hour of eating and drinking, the Cold War thawed and I returned to my Hotel enduring the disapproving stare of Boris who made it quite apparent he knew I had too much to drink.

The next morning I phoned Allan Schneider's cousin Luba, and when answered by a recorded voice, redialed several times. Consulting a Russian-English Dictionary I determined her number was Out-of-Order or disconnected. I debated the risk to Luba asking Boris to help me find her apartment. Certainly he reported on where I went and who I met. And certainly he was not subtle when he asked if I wanted to visit Moscow's only surviving Synagogue. I laughed at his clumsy attempt to find out what I was. Yes, I answered, I am Jewish and my father left Ekatrinislav in 1903 and I promise you I am not a Zionist Activist.

Boris grunted. He did not appreciate my sharp reply. "Where to now?" he asked as I relaxed in the back seat of his car. "The Taganka Theater, please."

Boris shook his head. Unhappy. Resigned. My request was out-of-bounds, Ill-advised. Unacceptable. No decent Soviet citizen or sympathetic visitor patronized the Taganka.

In my pocket, thanks to Allan Schneider's exuberance, was a letter of introduction to Yuri Lyubimov director of the Taganka and one of the world's most recognized masters of theatrical Art.

With flattering hyperbole Allan identified me as a promising playwright and a Droog or friend who would greatly benefit from seeing a Taganka production. Lyubimov escorted me to his office. That any Droog of Allan Schneider was a also Droog of Yuri's was instantly clear.

The white-painted walls of Lyubimov's office displayed congratulatory messages and signatures inscribed by the theatrical world's most famous performers, directors and playwrights. Laurence Olivier, Bertolt Brecht, Arthur Miller, John Osborn, Peter Weiss, and numerous other celebrated International visitors came to applaud and support this epicenter of freedom loving intellectuals who courageously kept alive amidst repression an audacious, sharp and independent view of Soviet society.

In 1982 as the Taganka's critical and thoughtful audience grew, the Nomenklatura's tolerance of dissent ended. Ignoring all International protests they deprived Yuri Lyubimov of his citizenship along with Alexander Solzhenitzen, Mstislav Rostropovitch, Joseph Brodsky and others and this great representative of Russian Art spent the next six years in forced emigration abroad.

That evening's performance of Yuri Lyubimov's production of Bertolt Brecht's "Galileo" was extraordinary. An overwhelming theatrical experience engaging my eye, ear and mind with every imaginable dramatic device and technique. Here was staging I had never seen before completely revising my concept of theater. Here, in the dark, on a cold winter's night in a Moscow suburb, Galileo's Inquisition came alive as heated and terrifying as one conducted by a modern Police State.

Seated beside me to translate the text a handsome, elderly actress beamed with delight when I said she resembled Madam Ouspenskya, a five-foot tall Russian Exile who ran a drama school in Hollywood. Aristocratic in face and bearing, my Translator spoke impeccable English whispering the play's dialogue in my ear with unrestrained passion.

For almost two hours we watched Galileo struggle against the relentless brutalities of Church and State. Nobility, courage and personal integrity gave way to a hopeless despair as, at the climax of a series of violent confrontations with established Doctrine, a truly great mind recanted its life's work. When the curtain came down the grief-stricken audience sat immobilized in the darkened theater, sobbing. Too drained of feeling to applaud.

They recognized that though hundreds of years distanced them from Galileo's tragic fate, nothing in contemporary life has changed. The Inquisition has not and will not ever end. Then, in an abrupt and amazing reversal of their despairing mood, on the darkened stage, illuminated by small circles of light, a chorus line of uniformed schoolboys suddenly appear, slowly walking towards the startled audience. Silently, step by step, the schoolboys walk forward, slowly rotating small Globes of the World on short sticks held out in front of them. Then the schoolboy vanish into sudden darkness, and when the small circles of light return, all we see are rows of slowly spinning Globes. Turning. Turning. Turning.

"You look like you need a drink," my Translator said as I sat frozen in my seat too overcome to do more than nod. Not often has my reaction to a great work of Art been so overwhelming. My intelligence, feelings, memory, and imagination were all stirred, crowding, jostling, overlapping one another making each moment on stage a violent personal experience.

"I know, I know," said my Translator recognizing my response to the play. "It can be too much. Unbearable the first time you see Galileo."

I nodded. And later, after a few Vodkas I confided my difficulty in finding Allan's cousin. My Translator rose from the table with my address book containing Luba's number and went to a phone. Five minutes later she returned smiling. Indeed laughing at me. "My Child," she said as if lecturing, "Her phone is not disconnected. Not Out-of-Order. Only changed. And here's the new number."

"Did you dial it?" I asked.

Her hand waved away my foolish question. "I did," she replied. "And?" I asked expectantly.

After a long and what actors call a pregnant pause my Translator replied: "It was busy."

I then asked her to phone again and set up a breakfast meeting at my Hotel tomorrow to receive Allan's letter. She nodded and graciously signified agreement with another imperial gesture reminding me of the diminutive Helen Hayes playing the Czarina in "Anastasia". For some actors all of life is a performance and they are forever on-stage or on-camera. My Translator was more than delighted with her role and I, her only audience, dared not applaud. Her only reward was three or four more Vodkas which miraculously did not impair her Regal bearing or the clarity of her speech as she returned from the phone several times explaining without disappointment or the slightest trace of impatience: "Still busy. Still busy."

Finally, an hour later, she returned from the phone and said in a low conspiratorial voice: "It is done. 9 A.M. Tomorrow."

At breakfast Luba arrived without her husband who was on duty at their Hospital. Astonished by the letter and Visa applications, she read them carefully shaking her head and then looking at me convinced I was aware of and agreed with Allan's advice. After the waiter served coffee, toast and eggs, Luba glanced around the dining room to insure no one could possibly hear what she was about to say.

"Allan is such a romantic," she declared affectionately. "He believes he's rescuing Aristocrats from the Guillotine. He doesn't understand our situation. My husband and I are respected doctors, well-paid, with a large apartment, shop in privileged stores with good pensions to look forward to. Why should we leave Russia?"

I hesitated a moment before asking "What about your son?" Luba put down Allan's letter and stirred her coffee a moment before replying. "He made a dreadful mistake. The government was educating him to be a Doctor for Russia. Not for Israel. He was a Zionist. A Cosmopolitan. And then when they discharged him from Medical School he over-reacted and now we must all learn to live with what he did to himself. Tell Allan that, please."

Allan asked me to be persuasive. To encourage his cousins to emigrate. However I said nothing recalling the ultimate fate of German Jews who could not be persuaded to abandon their homes and furniture in the years preceding the "Final Solution". Luba and her husband believed they had everything. Everything but Freedom, and I was not about to attempt to change their minds. After a moment of silence I asked: "What about anti-Semitism?"

Luba laughed. "To most Russians we will always be Yids. That will never change. We live with it every day. But nevertheless we are valued and rewarded by

the government for what we do. Not for who we are."
For the next hour I answered Luba's questions about
Allan. His family and career. Life in Dobbs Ferry.
And what did I think of Moscow? Innocent small talk
avoiding the unmentionable subject of Emigration.
We hugged and kissed as we parted and when she
walked out of the Hotel I was convinced I would
never see Luba again.

After breakfast, a few minutes walk from my Hotel
to Red Square, I often visited the War Memorial
to the 27 million Russians killed in "The Great
Patriotic War". In a city that seemed inhabited only
with unhappy frozen-faced citizens in thick woolen
overcoats and fur hats, this Nation's Shrine to the
dead alone seemed to affirm the joy of being alive
in Russia today. Arriving in Taxis from the Marriage
Bureau young, newly-wed couples solemnly placed
their flower bouquets at the base of the monument
in a moving ceremony that pledged their lives to the
memory of all who had fallen to make this joyous
day possible. Like Washington's Vietnam Wall, this
Memorial exposed the heartache of a wounded nation
expressing a grief that will forever be beyond words.

On my last day in Moscow Boris asked: "Why do
you visit the Memorial?"

I said nothing. Surprised by his question. "Did you
lose someone in war?" he asked. "Several friends and
a brother," I said in no mood for any conversation.

"I lost my family. Everyone," Boris said without
a trace of Russian melancholy in his face or voice.
"I'm sorry," I answered acknowledging his loss with
a sympathetic nod. "Were you in the Army?" Boris
asked.

"The Navy."

Boris grinned. "I should have known. From your coat," he explained. "I was at Stalingrad," he continued, lowering his voice. "Stalingrad."

"Yes," I answered, without encouraging further comment.

"Do you know Stalingrad?" Boris asked.

I nodded. "Yes. I know about Stalingrad. You killed half a million Nazis. Captured 98 thousand. And ten years later less than five thousand returned to Germany."

Boris was for a moment, speechless. "How do you know that?" he demanded.

"From History books."

"It's the truth," he replied, turning in his seat to look at me for the first time pleased by something I said.

"And we also know you destroyed more of the German Army than any other country in the war."

"That's also true," Boris said proudly. "A well-known fact."

Boris remained silent for a few minutes. Thinking. There was no guessing what was on his mind. "What hour is your Flight?" he asked.

"Eight P.M."

Boris stared at me. Hesitating. "How would you like to see the real Russia?" he asked.

"I've already seen it."

"No!" he insisted. "Moscow is not the real Russia. The real Russia is way out there!" With a sweep of his arm he pointed down the broad avenue leading past the airport and to the outskirts of the city.

After checking out of the Hotel and loading my baggage into his car, we drove for more than an hour to a small roadside Inn on the Steppes of his beloved

Mother Russia. In all directions, extending to the far horizon, we were surrounded and overwhelmed by a vista of a limitless and placid sea of farmland. One feels powerless confronted by such emptiness. Boris was right. I thanked him for showing me that the Steppes and not the cities are the real Russia. Here could be seen the devastating power that swallowed the Armies of Napoleon and Hitler.

Our long lunch washed down with the kindest, most gentle no-hangover potato Vodka I have ever tasted revealed one more surprise. When I complimented Boris on his excellent English he disclosed he had once been the Russian Ambassador's driver in Washington and proudly related his memory of the District's fabulous Sea Food restaurants as well as his passion for Chesapeake Crab Cakes.

That evening at the Airport we said goodbye with a brief hug in traditional Russian style. Then the astonishing speed with which Boris escorted me through Customs and Passport Control made unmistakably clear he was more than a regular Intourist chauffeur assigned to drive just another curious Tourist.

Hopefully, I'd like to believe on that final day of our often unpleasant encounter we became Druzya. Friends.

Six months later, answering the doorbell of my Palisades Avenue home, I was greeted by Allan and his delighted cousin Luba. The Nomenklatura's expanding paranoia had made life difficult for the Schneiders after a series of Show Trials falsely convicted several Jewish Doctors of poisoning high-ranking members of the Politburo. Luba arrived on a

Visitor's Visa to explore the possibility of continuing her medical career in the United States. Her husband would also defect if they could find work as doctors. A hope that Allan encouraged with little doubt that his brilliant cousins had much to offer American Medicine. A false hope. The Iron Curtain of the American Medical Community could not be breached without enduring another Residency, and Internship, and passing State licensing exams. After six months of unsuccessful job interviews Luba's Visa expired and she returned to Moscow.

A year later, rehearsing a new production in London, Allan stepped out of the theater and crossing the street to mail a letter was knocked down by a careless motorcyclist. Badly injured, Allan died the next day.

For many months after his funeral I continued to look for Allan on the 1:10 from Dobbs Ferry to Grand Central. Certainly another false hope riding a train that often seemed haunted. I still have no doubt that Allan's joyful exuberance and enormous talent will forever live in the memory of all who knew him as a friend, teacher, and gifted director.

Shakespeare's Horatio spoke for us all when he said: "Good night Sweet Prince."

PRAGUE

In 1976 Prague's InterContinental Hotel was an exotic Alfred Hitchcock movie set crowded with foreign characters in Turbans, Saris and baggy business suits. Russian, Chinese and North Korean Purchasing Commissions seemed permanent residents enjoying the rich food and entertaining night life of a magnificent city that had everything to offer a civilized man but Freedom.

Socialism With A Human Face, the Spring of 68's Democratic Charter had been defeated by Russian Tanks, and only the irrepressible Czech talent for satire and hope alleviated the despair all Patriots felt for their nation's unhappy fate.

Seated in a comfortable armchair across from the Telex desk waiting for messages, I looked out at the hotel's Lobby and witnessed an amusing demonstration of bureaucratic politics. Officials at different levels of power and authority deferred to each other by bowing and shaking hands before sitting on overstuffed Lounge chairs to drink startling quantities of Vodka and good Scotch whiskey.

"Count the Fountain pens displayed in their breast pockets," the Telex Operator whispered to me. "The one with the most Fountain pens is always the Boss."

I suppressed a laugh. And, as the only American in the hotel that cold winter day, I certainly felt conspicuous by my clothing and manner. Which explained why no one but this middle-aged Telex Operator dared be friendly. She congratulated me on my wife's reassuring messages from New York saying that our newborn son was thriving and not to worry as my adolescent daughter was now behaving herself.

I congratulated her on her impeccable English. "I do miss England," she said, explaining how much she enjoyed her war-time job as secretary with the Czech Government-in-Exile in London. Studying the crowded Lobby for a moment she turned to me, smiled and rolled her eyes. "Just like George Orwell's 'Animal Farm' don't you think?"

I nodded, returned her smile, and without answering began writing a reply to my wife. On my arrival at Prague and checking in at the American Embassy, the Commercial Attaché gave me a Guide book titled: "Security Suggestions for U.S. Businessmen Abroad" describing the risk in responding to negative political comments. Entrapment by Provocateurs and costly fines and prison were a real threat to Americans working behind the Iron Curtain during the Cold War. "Loose lips can do more than sink ships," this State Department booklet advised reviving a familiar war time slogan.

I am sure my silent rebuff of her comment disappointed the Telex Operator eager to talk to English-speaking visitors and no doubt my government-induced Paranoia limited my ability to distinguish an innocent friend from a devious foe.

Despite the recent bombing and destruction of the popular books and magazines available at our USIS Library, the Czech government's wall, designed to keep out Decadent Western Culture, did have a hole which I hoped to penetrate. Our Consulate's Commercial Attaché insisted any attempt to induce ORT, the regions Telecommunication Network to participate in a multi-national Satellite Broadcast was Quixotic. Any program not originated by the Government would never be aired.

Nevertheless the ORT Officials were enthusiastic. They were fascinated by the idea of broadcasting programs world-wide by Satellite. In 1976 the Pope's Christmas Message and Mohammad Ali's Championship fights had reached millions of viewers.

Without haggling, they agreed to link their East European Micro-Wave transmissions with West Europe's Eurovision network, down-linking a multi-national Satellite feed extending from Moscow to New York, including twelve Central and South American Cities. The World Health Organization's Hypertension Program would start off with a Big Bang. It would be spectacular. I felt like a candidate for Broadcasting's Hall of Fame. With Russia's Cardiology Institute interacting with our National Institutes of Health, all political obstacles to sharing leading edge scientific knowledge would now be circumvented.

The one unpleasant aspect of that day-long ORT meeting was the non-stop eating and drinking of Vodka, Caviar, Blini and thick meat sandwiches which one American diplomat described as a calculated attack on the effete Western Gall Bladder. Thankfully there were no Toasts with glasses raised between rounds of drinks. I do believe there emerged something more than pro forma gestures of good will with several suggestions that even members of the Nomenclatura are decent human beings despite Party Line propaganda broadcasts from either side of the Iron Curtain.

I have no idea how later that evening I returned to the InterContinental. I vaguely remember the Doorman helping me from my Taxi into the hotel where a waiter brought me a pot of steaming black coffee.

The tall impressive Doorman, a Danny Kaye look-alike, wore a resplendent uniform with star-studded epaulets, gold braid and a row of military decorations across his broad chest. The "scrambled eggs" on the visor of his cap would evoke envy in a Four Star Admiral, and whenever I arrived or departed from the hotel he stamped his heels on the ground British Army style, came to attention and saluted.

I always returned my finest Pensacola Naval Cadet salute, elbow out to one side, rigid fingers raised to my forehead before snapping my hand down with a great show of respect.

He always grinned at me and one day winked an eye and I felt I had made a friend.

By the time I finished my pot of coffee the only other Westerner at the InterContinental arrived after a joyous night carousing in a Cabaret. A bottle of Champagne in his hand he staggered to my table and insisted on drinking with me. A short pear-shaped Dutchman, he seemed a jolly old Elf, a salesman for Philips who when discovering my wife was born in Amsterdam declared his great admiration for all Americans in general and me in particular. After all, who won the war and liberated Holland. Yes?

After several glasses of Champagne, now well past midnight, the Doorman came in from the street and locked the front door. The Dutchman jumped to his feet and roaring like a Prussian Drill Sergeant shouted across the empty lobby at the Doorman who stiffened to attention. The Dutchman turned to me and asked: "Would you like to see how a Russian General Goose Steps?"

I nodded. He barked another command. The Doorman reversed the visor on his cap, pointing it backwards, stamped one heel on the Lobby floor, and as the Dutchman shouted cadence LEFT! RIGHT! LEFT! RIGHT! LEFT! RIGHT! did an exaggerated Goose Step across the lobby leaning back as he marched, straight legs raised up and out to the level of his waist in a remarkable display of flexibility and balance.

Arriving at the wall at the far end of the Lobby, responding to the Dutchman's shouted command RIGHT ABOUT TURN!, the Doorman pivoted on one leg while swinging the other behind his back, kicking the reversed cap off his head. The cap tumbled up and forward through the air. Without missing a count in his Goose Stepping stride, the Doorman reached up, caught the cap and placed it properly on his head, the "scrambled egg" visor now pointing in the direction of his march across the Lobby.

The Dutchman roared with delight. I applauded and then respectfully saluted as the Doorman joined us in finishing the Champagne.

The next morning, at a late breakfast, while attempting to repair the consequences of yesterday's intemperance a distinguished elderly gentleman, carrying a large Manila envelope asked permission to share my table. He introduced himself with a slight European bow and I welcomed him as possible relief from my hangover. After ordering his meal he asked if I was interested in Postage stamps.

I replied I was once an avid Collector. He then showed me a sheet of stamps explaining that these were rare and although printed eight years ago had never been issued. In fact most had been destroyed when the present Communist regime revised the official History of the Czechoslovakian Jews. During brief months of freedom in the Spring of '68 a more democratic government recognized and honored with these stamps the Czechoslovakian Jews deported to Concentration Camps. After Russian Tanks occupied King Wenceslas Square, the previous policy resumed. Jews were now considered no different from other citizens murdered by the Nazis.

Holocaust victims were now identified as anti-Fascist Czech patriots. The fact that they were Jews had nothing to do with their fate.

"Would I perhaps be interested in a few stamps?" he asked. "For your collection," he said, smiling.

I nodded. "How much?"

"One hundred dollars."

I poured myself another cup of coffee and remained silent. The old Gentleman paused a moment carefully spooning and then salting a hard-boiled egg. He shook his head evaluating my show of indifference. "Perhaps seventy-five dollars? Yes?"

I said nothing. Ignoring his offer. The old Gentleman laughed. He looked up, raising his eyes as if talking to an unseen presence hovering over our table. "A Landsman?" he said with a sigh.

"Of course," I replied.

Resigned to making a bad bargain he held out a hand. "Only for you," he said. "Only for you. I want you should have these stamps no matter the price. Fifty dollars? Yes?"

I nodded. He handed me his card and again introduced himself as the unofficial Mayor of Prague's elderly Jewish Community supervising the Restaurant at the Senior Citizen's Residence around the corner from the "Alter Schule", the centuries old Synagogue where Rabbi Loew, author of "The Golem" was buried. "You must come to my office," he insisted. "I'm on the Second floor, above the restaurant," he explained. "I would like you to see our Archives."

"You're a Historian?" I asked.

"Not really. Just an Archivist."

"What do you collect?"

He smiled his charming smile and rose from the table. "More than Postage stamps," he said.

I explained I was due at the Airport at Noon tomorrow and doubted I would have time to see his Archives. "Make the time," he insisted. "My office opens at 9."

The next morning I knocked on an office door marked: "ARCHIV" and entered a room about the size of a Basketball Court crowded with parallel rows of waist high tables displaying what at first I believed to be extra-long shoe boxes all the same color. Green. Arranged alphabetically the open boxes contained hand-written and properly tabbed Index Cards each one rubber-stamped with an official Swastika Seal.

The old Gentleman, The Mayor, approached with a pencil and writing pad in one hand and without saying a word I followed him to the far corner of the room to a table marked with a large "W." "Here," he said, handing me the pencil and pad. "Maybe here you will find what you are looking for." He nodded at an open box of Cards, reached up and gently patted my cheek as if to wish me luck. Then he turned, walked away and left me alone.

I thumbed through the file of Cards written in legible Germanic script detailing the name, address, date of birth, occupation, education, religion, and ultimate fate of each victim Transported or Relocated to the Slave Labor and Extermination Camps at Auschwitz. Also recorded was the date, number and Assembly Point of the Railroad Transport that carried that individual to their doom.

What was I doing here? What was I searching for? What power guided my hand and eye compelling me to read through this large file of Index Cards? Was I perhaps looking for my own name?

Half way through the file, I pulled out a Card and held the answer to my questions and my quest in my hand. "Rebecca Rose Weissman. Age 94. Auschwitz" the Card said.

My Vienna-born Grandmother's name was Rebecca Rose Weissman, a name given to my daughter to honor a remarkable woman who came to the United States about Nineteen hundred, and died at 94 at my Parent's home in Brooklyn. With a Weissman marrying an unrelated Weissman, over several generations, Rebecca Rose became a traditional family name very much alive today.

But not this Rebecca Rose, who may or may not have been my relation. Shocked, dismayed, I slid the Card back into the file and like someone possessed, fled towards the office door. Rushing away, perhaps denying something I did not understand.

The Old Gentleman, The Mayor, stopped me at the door. He took my hand as if to comfort me. In a moment I calmed down and thanked him. "I must get to the Airport," I said. "I must not miss my plane."

He nodded and smiled his most charming smile accented with a slight old-fashioned bow. In a soft voice, almost a whisper, he asked: "Perhaps you would like to make a small donation to the Archive? Yes?"

I turned away, rushing to the stairs, leaving behind a room filled with hand-written records of horrors the world can no longer deny.

My wild, life-threatening Taxi ride to the airport was unnecessary. The runways were shrouded in fog. No flights were arriving or departing. I checked my luggage and went to the Bar. I had more to think about than I could deal with. The Postage stamps. The Cards. The Names. What exactly was happening? Who was this charming Mayor with his fantastic Archive? Was he a Con Man living off vulnerable Tourists? If so he was obscene. Personally trading on sorrow. Exploiting a human tragedy that defies understanding. But then perhaps he is a man with a Mission? Someone driven by an obligation to remember? To compel others to remember?

My confused thoughts were interrupted by drunken shouting at the other end of the Bar. I questioned the

Bartender who explained the uproar. The Chief Pilot of the Airline was venting rage at Management who only allow him to schedule but never fly planes. As a Fighter pilot with the Czech Squadron of the RAF, and a decorated national hero, he was untouchable by intimidated Supervisors resigned to endure his verbal abuse.

"Fooking God Damn Government!" he shouted again and again. "Fooking God Damn Pig-headed Commissars don't know nothing! Never learn nothing!" Lecturing several other stranded and intoxicated passengers, his curriculum consisted of the evils of Socialist mismanagement washed down with gallons of Pilsner Beer and Russian Vodka.

"Now I've heard everything," I said.

"No you haven't," the Bartender replied, explaining the Chief Pilot had been invited to play the Organ at the re-dedication of the re-built Coventry Cathedral in England and the government refused to allow him to leave the country.

"Afraid he would defect?"

"No! Not at all. He loves raising Hell here. They're afraid he'll get drunk, botch the performance and embarrass our country."

"He plays the Organ?"

"He was a Church Organist as a boy. And when Coventry was destroyed in 1940, he was stationed at a nearby RAF Base and worked with other Servicemen to rescue hundreds of people out of the rubble. All that survived the bombing was a wall of the Cathedral and the Organ. So he sat down and played for several hours. That was how he kept from going crazy he told reporters who interviewed him afterwards. Last month the British gave him a Medal and an invitation to come to Coventry and play again."

The Chief Pilot ended his rant with sullen silence. The other stranded passengers drifted from the Bar. It would be several hours before the fog lifted. The Chief Pilot then walked over as if in search of an audience. Studying the Passenger Manifest in his hand he found my name.

"You must be the American," he said.

"Yes."

"How did you like Prague?"

"Beautiful. Good people. A few laughs."

"Don't you know better than to talk to Bartenders?" he asked. "They're all Informers."

The Bartender shook his head wagging one finger signaling not to reply.

"What did he tell you about me?"

"Not much."

"Did he tell you about Elizabeth the Queen of England who was a Princess during the war driving a Lorry?"

"No."

"Well one day the Lorry wouldn't start and when she raised the hood to check the engine I came over to help. Three Secret Service Bodyguards grabbed me, and when I resisted, not knowing who they were , they gave me a bad time. Beat me up. Did he tell you about that?"

"No."

"All Governments are the same. They're all no damn good."

When I nodded agreement his hostility vanished. He bought me another Beer.

"Were you in the War?"

"Navy Pilot."

He was impressed. Friendly. "Tell me," he asked. "Do you still have your Flying Boots? Those beautiful Sheepskin leather American boots. The only boots that ever kept my feet warm."

"They're long gone," I said. "Stolen."

"Mine were also stolen. We've become a nation of thieves. The government robs us and now we steal from each other." Paranoia flickered across my Radar. The Chief Pilot was no drunken fool. I finished my drink ignoring his statement.

"I tell you what," he said. "When you're home buy me a pair and I'll pay you. What do you say?"

"No problem," I said. "Be happy to send them to you."

And so, several drinks later, after hearing about shooting down German ME 109's, the Fog lifted and I returned to New York and mailed him a pair of Flying boots.

For many years his Thank You card hung on my office wall. A Cartoon titled: "RUSSIA'S SECRET WEAPON" showing a large War Elephant with Spears protruding from the nostrils of an upraised Trunk. Between his rear legs a pair of enormous testicles lay on an iron Anvil. A resplendent uniformed Russian Field Marshall stood poised next to the testicles with a Hammer raised high, ready to strike a heavy blow launching two primitive spears at an unseen enemy.

Some pictures do indeed say more than a thousand words. Yes?

THANKSGIVING

Primary Flight Training at Naval Air Station Bunker Hill, Peru, Indiana, consisted of four months of twelve hour days surviving a rigorous flying and ground-school curriculum that preceded six months of Advanced Training at Pensacola. Located sixty miles north of Indianapolis on several thousand treeless acres, Bunker Hill overlooked a depressed landscape of abandoned farms, unpainted farmhouses and dilapidated barns unaffected by wartime prosperity. Without conventional runways, Bunker Hill's airport was a three thousand foot circular paved field that enabled six or more planes to take-off and land simultaneously. Despite our worst fears, accidents were rare though we shared that intimidating landing area with a contingent of Royal Navy Cadets who somehow lacked our self-confident "hot pilot" attitude.

In the six months following Pearl Harbor on abandoned prairie farmland the Navy erected double-decker wooden Barracks, Classrooms, an Administration Building, a Mess hall, a Movie Theater, and a bowling alley. Three Airplane Hangers, enormous all-wood buildings adjacent to the Flight Line of several hundred Stearman training planes were a remarkable construction achievement during a bitter Indiana winter. And to our dismay, on our arrival the following November, our Meteorology Instructor enjoyed informing Cadets only a single strand of barbed wire at the Canadian border stood between Bunker Hill and the frigid arctic air flowing down from the North Pole.

A dire forecast of future suffering not to be ignored. Two daily ninety minute open-cockpit flights with a chill factor of thirty below could only be endured wearing long-johns, heavy woolen trousers and shirt, a thick woolen sweater under a sheepskin lined leather bib overall and flight jacket. A face mask, helmet and thick leather gloves enabled me to survive the 30/30 rule stating that at thirty below zero human flesh froze in thirty seconds.

Ready Rooms where we warmed ourselves between flights provided hot coffee and doughnuts thanks to the generosity of local citizens who welcomed Naval Cadets into their community. With sons and husbands overseas, the mothers and wives of nearby Kokomo and Logansport began knitting with a patriotic fervor that provided an unlimited supply of woolen sweaters and Balaclavas freely distributed by the Red Cross.

A Balaclava is a woolen hood covering head and neck exposing only the eyes. Worn under my helmet, face mask and goggles, a Balaclava enabled me to fly without freezing my face. Severe frostbite was the inevitable penalty for the unprotected, so I appreciated this gift and wrote to thank the woman who knitted it.

In beautiful hand-written calligraphy the card in the box the Balaclava came in advised me to stay warm and safe. The sender also suggested I visit her when hungry for a good home-cooked meal. Cadets usually declined these generous invitations for with Liberty restricted to Saturday afternoons and Sunday, the exotic lures of Chicago and Indianapolis were usually a greater attraction.

I did however receive and reply to several other letters from my wartime pen-pal who told me she had been knitting since December 7th and intended to continue until the war ended or her supply of yarn was exhausted. Later, her Balaclava kept me warm when skiing, reminding me for more than twenty years that I missed an opportunity to learn about someone I knew nothing about. I still wonder about the woman with the beautiful calligraphy. Was she married? A Widow? An Old Maid? Did she ever run out of yarn? How many garments did she knit during the war? How many home-cooked meals did she serve to more appreciative Cadets? Nagging questions that taught me something about myself.

Yes. Missed learning opportunities never come again. And I did miss many such experiences. At eighteen I was shy, though filled with absolute certainties, inhabiting a closed circle of knowledge about people and the lives they led. I simply did not know how to cope with this woman's uncomplicated generosity because I did not then realize that Brooklyn and Indiana are not so different. Sharing identical values of family, love and religion. Experiencing similar thoughts and feelings. To break-out of my narrow self-limiting world would become a never-ending task that perhaps began my first Thanksgiving away from home in a wealthy mansion in Indiana.

A notice posted on the Mess Hall's Bulletin Board invited 20 Aviation Cadets to sign up for a Bus trip to Indianapolis to share Thanksgiving with twenty Junior League debutantes all of good families, an event arranged by our Chaplain attempting to divert lustful young men from the fleshpots of the Midwest. And so despite our preference for the enthusiastic amateurs encountered at the Indiana Roof Ballroom, or the Hotel Claypool, more than twenty adventurous Cadets signed up. An opportunity to go Off-Base on a Thursday would be a break in our grueling training routine as well as a welcome relief from Navy cooking.

In an affluent Indianapolis suburb the mansion that welcomed us belonged to the city's wealthiest family now crowded with eager nubile Junior Leaguers, look-alike flowers doing their bit to win the war. The dinner was excellent, though alcohol free, the conversation polite, and the Cadets from various economic backgrounds properly subdued by good manners in an environment of conspicuous wealth.

No one relaxed or had fun until Glenn Miller, Tommy Dorsey and Benny Goodman records began playing and we escaped from the polite and boring conversation at the table to begin dancing. And dance we did from energetic Jitterbugging to Fox Trots to slow moving romantic shuffles with our bodies pressed not too close as we were dutifully observed by parental Chaperones. Our Hostess, the high-spirited Lady of the House was slim, well-preserved, decorously dressed in a full-length white evening gown that gave no hint of her age. She danced non-stop, randomly selecting partners determined that everyone, no matter how shy or inept a dancer should have a good time. She was a living embodiment of the cliché "the life of the party" successfully competing with young Junior League girls for our attention.

When she asked me to dance I did not hesitate surprised at how my dancing improved with an experienced partner who smoothly flowed with the enticing slow throb of Glenn Miller's Star Dust melodies. Though it was no time for conversation my charming Hostess dutifully asked my name, where I was from, and after a thoughtful pause she said: "That's a Jewish name, I believe?"

"Yes," I said. "Definitely."

My Hostess immediately flushed with embarrassment. Apologized. Eager to explain herself. "Please don't misunderstand," she pleaded. "I thought maybe you might be Catholic."

We continued dancing while I tried coping with the thought I was more acceptable to my Hostess as a Jew than as a Catholic. A total reversal of everything I had learned in Brooklyn. "It seems," she continued, "that most of the other Cadets here today are Catholic."

"That's true," I said. Aware of it for the first time. "Most of them are from Boston," I explained. "There are a lot of Catholics in Boston, you know."

She shrugged, made a wry face as if to say - that's life. An unpleasant fact we all had to bear with - and she seemed to assume I shared her prejudiced feelings.

My Hostess then named all her close Jewish friends, wealthy contributors to Indianapolis' rich cultural life, specifically by bringing to the Midwest the internationally famous conductor Fabian Sevitsky who transformed the local symphony into a recognized classical orchestra. "You know he's the brother of Serge Koussevitsky of the Boston Symphony," she said. "Fabian shortened his name for professional reasons."

"Yes, I do know about that," I replied. "My brother studied one summer at Tanglewood with Serge Koussevitsky."

My Hostess stopped dancing. Stared at me a moment. Smiled her most enchanting smile. I thought she was about to kiss me. "I think it is just wonderful," she said beaming with approval, "How you people love music."

I never saw my bigoted Hostess again. And I did enjoy the Saturday night Fabian Sevitsky concerts of the Indianapolis Symphony free to servicemen with ninety-nine per cent of the audience definitely not Jewish. During my four months in Indiana I also learned about the Klu Klux Klan, the anti-Catholic anti-black organization that dominated Indiana's social and political life. The Klan wielded a more subtle and powerful influence than what could be achieved by cross burnings and masked parades. KKK spread it's insidious virus of hate poisoning schools, newspaper editorials, Protestant Churches and the State government. Not limited to poor ignorant "Rednecks", the KKK was an effective means of getting and retaining political and economic power by attractive, well-educated, and otherwise respectable community leaders like my hostess.

I never did ask our Navy Chaplain why from the long list of Cadets signing up for that memorable

Thanksgiving dinner he selected nineteen Catholics and one Jew. Was he making a statement? Fighting prejudice? Teaching tolerance? Or merely having fun? He was a popular and jolly old Priest who seemed to smile and laugh as often as he prayed. I regret I never did ask. And so my question remains unanswered. Another missed opportunity to learn something more about my world.

FLYING

The monthly issues of FLYING magazine were an exciting purchase for a schoolboy seeking adventure. For twenty-five cents fascinating articles and photographs delivered more thrills and chills than a fifty cent Saturday matinee at King Highway's Avalon Theater. Fearless Aviators crossing oceans and exploring ice-covered continents stoked my interest in flying's heroic pioneers. And to my delight I could see them and their airplanes less than a half hour from my East 28th street home.

Wearing an Aviator's helmet and leather gloves and pulling the goggles down over my eyes I bicycled every Saturday to Floyd Bennett Airport where I learned to identify Stinson Reliants, stagger wing Beechcrafts, Wacos, Aeroncas and Piper Cubs circling the field with reliability and skill that confirmed my determination to someday learn to fly.

My interest in collecting foreign postage stamps waned as I devoted after-school hours building a model of a Curtis Dive bomber. My amazed father considered it an exact replica and fearing its destruction would not allow me to fly it. Instead he hung it from the ceiling of our summer Bunkhouse unaware it was a precursor of his son's future in the sky. A future dramatized in such popular movies as *Hells Angels*, *Dawn Patrol* and *All Quiet on the Western Front.*

My enthusiasm to watch airplanes led me to bicycle thirty miles to Port Washington, Long Island to see the Pan American Airways Boeing Flying Boats depart for Southampton, England. An exhausting but satisfying ride for the Big Story of the 1930's was aviation's startling progress dramatized in headlines and on the radio. Amelia Earhart and Howard Hughes' around-the-world flights were daily newspaper Cliffhangers and when Earhart disappeared in the South Pacific the search for her plane rivaled the hunt for the kidnapped Lindbergh baby as our nation's first great media Blitz.

Of greater interest were the Lindbergh's Trans-Atlantic route-finding flights detailed in National Geographic articles written by Anne Morrow Lindbergh who poetically described her husband's devotion to his quest to make commercial air travel a reality. The routes they pioneered in a small single engine sea plane became Pan American Airways world-wide network of scheduled flights that by 1938 were routine.

The Lindbergh's were Gurus of aviation. Eloquent forecasters of a promising future that included recognition of the destructive potential of air power. In 1938, returning from Nazi Germany, Lindbergh, an honored and decorated guest of that government described invincible Squadrons of German Bombers foretelling cities reduced to rubble by an irresistible

94

force that would soon overwhelm Europe's peace-loving Democracies.

Lindbergh became a persuasive spokesman for the "America First" political movement - Isolationists advocating America stay out of foreign wars - remain neutral - deny all military and financial aid to England now fighting for survival. Morally blind to the evil of Hitler, Lindbergh repeated Nazi justifications for their brutal attempt to conquer Europe and Russia. "To return civilization to a new dark ages" as Winston Churchill said.

Lindbergh replied at an "America First" political rally saying on national radio: "America has no interest in a war that only serves the interest of England and the Jews."

Denounced by President Roosevelt as a traitor to all freedom-loving Democracies, Lindbergh resigned his Air Force Commission and was not permitted to re-enlist after Pearl Harbor. Our national hero was now an anti-semite whose wife wrote *The Wave of The Future* arguing that a totalitarian world was inevitable. Democracy was finished, she predicted. Government's of - by - and for the People was a naive fantasy. Man is incapable of self-rule and will always need the strong virile leadership of Dictators.

Other more admirable heroes, one thousand Royal Air Force Pilots, captured the world's attention and were immortalized by Winston Churchill when he said: "Never in the history of human conflict has so much been owed by so many to so few."

The young Pilots defending England the summer of 1940, smiling into newsreel cameras after each victorious flight, won the hearts and minds of everyone aware of what they were fighting and dying for. The survival of human decency.

When in 1942 I brought my application to enlist as a Naval Aviation Cadet to my mother for signature, she did not argue. She was aware of my feelings and approved of what I wanted. Opening a Bible on our dining room table she placed the papers on it and overcoming her fears, without comment, signed with what I now realize was great courage. My brother Bernard had been flying in the Navy the past year and she would now have two sons to worry about until the war ended.

Somewhere in Aviators Heaven teaching Angels to fly is my first Flight Instructor, an old-time civilian pilot Herbert W. Arnold of Lancaster, Pennsylvania. Unlike many Navy Instructors venting their frustration at an unwelcome teaching assignment by shouting at terrified Cadets, Arnold never raised his voice. In fact, he was devoted to sharing his love of flying with Cadets repeating over the "Voice tube" that was our only Intercom such aphorisms as - "Look around and live!" - and when encouraging frozen-faced students to lean back and relax he happily recited the statement on the sign posted over the door of our Ready Room - "There are Old Pilots and there are Bold Pilots. But there are - No Old Bold Pilots."

I learned to fly in an open-cockpit fabric covered Bi-plane built in 1923 at the Naval Aircraft factory in Philadelphia. The Instructor and Cadet sat behind a Wright Cyclone 235 horsepower engine started with a hand crank that raised a sweat on the coldest days. Painted yellow to identify a training plane and called

"The Yellow Peril", the upper and lower wings were braced by a maze of struts and wires.

At cruising speed the air flowing over these bracing wires produced a high-pitched hum, and, as you slowed and approached stalling speed, the wires sang in descending order the notes of an old Hymn - "Nearer My God to Thee."

Humming this tune, with or without religious fervor, Arnold's students consistently made bounce-free landings envied by other Cadets unaware of this old Pilot's secret.

Arnold taught his students to love the roar of the engine, the pungent smell of hot oil, the cool air flowing over our faces and the humming of the wires; what was called since the Wright Brothers and what is now no longer taught - the art of "Flying by the seat of your pants."

An art that combined all our physical senses to produce the feeling of flight and today, sitting strapped in a seat at forty thousand feet crossing oceans in a modern Jet I think of the pilots up front surrounded by a maze of electronic monitors who must be encouraged to take their eyes off the instruments to occasionally look out the window.

Lieutenant George Dickey, my next Flight Instructor, replaced Herbert Arnold's love of flying and humorous poetry with a relentless demand for precision. He was a by-the-book Naval Officer considered too old for combat who expected nothing less than one hundred per cent performance from students. Formation flying, Loops, Slow Rolls, Wing-overs and Spins were our daily curriculum and you had to recover from a three-turn Spin at exactly three turns. Two and two thirds or three and a quarter turns earned you a Down check and after three consecutive Downs you were washed out of Flight Training. He was respectfully called "Downcheck Dickey" by Cadets who thought themselves fortunate to have him as an Instructor because unlike other sadistic Officers he never wrung-out Cadets with a wild series of aerobatic maneuvers designed to separate the men from the boys by inducing air sickness.

In an unusually severe Indiana winter, training in an open-cockpit Stearman Bi-plane wearing a face mask, goggles, heavy leather sheepskin-lined jacket, bib overalls, boots, and thick flying gloves I sweated-out every flight. After flying several hours exposed to a wind chill factor of twenty below, I hurried to my Locker after each "hop" to take off my sweat-soaked woolen Long-Johns and thick sweater and hopefully dry them before my next flight in the frigid air.

"Downcheck Dickey" was the most professional pilot I ever flew with. Controlled. Precise. A vivid demonstration of the maxim - "You make it by working at it all the time."

Late one winter afternoon practicing precision power-off landings to a hundred foot circle at an outlying field thirty miles North of Bunker Hill's Main Station, we were enveloped in a heavy blizzard "Whiteout". There was no horizon. No visibility. We were flying inside a milk bottle in a plane not equipped for instrument flying.

Fortunately the highway from Logansport to Indianapolis was somewhere below, and leaning out of the cockpit Lieutenant Dickey dove down to the tree tops on either side of the road following the snow covered highway at an altitude of no more than thirty feet to guide us back to Bunker Hill.

Climbing out of the cockpit and walking to the Hanger Lieutenant Dickey patted me on the shoulder and for the first time I saw his long, austere face soften into a broad smile.

He turned to me and nodded. "Great fun, wasn't it?" he said, laughing.

I nodded, smiling my most fearless smile, saluted, and walked to my Locker as fast as possible to get out of my sweat-soaked Long-Johns.

A Front seat cross-country solo flight was a "Rite of Passage" for Cadets successfully completing Primary Training. In 148 hours flying time all my flights had been flown from the rear seat with or without an Instructor in front, and all my cross-country flying was in formations of three planes with Cadets alternately leading the Flight on each of three legs or course changes. With a heavy sandbag strapped in the back seat to reproduce the weight of a passenger, and with a full load of fuel, flying from the front seat was the best of all possible graduation presents. For the first time I truly felt I had grown wings. I selected my destination. Checked the weather. Plotted my course allowing for head winds and drift. Estimated fuel consumption, time of arrival, and filed a Flight Plan.

I had read about the beautiful sand dunes on Lake Michigan's shores and chose Benton Harbor as my destination. My route had highly visible "checkpoints" at half-hour intervals, enabling me to continuously correct my course for wind drift. I estimated two hours and forty five minutes flying time with a half hour of fuel in reserve. To add to my joy it was the first day of Spring. The freshly plowed farms below had just been manured, and from an altitude of one thousand feet I saw the landscape turning green after a long hard winter.

Pilots flying cross-country before the introduction of electronic OMNI Beacons and Air Traffic Controllers, relied on the names of towns painted on rooftops, water towers, farm silos and railroad stations to locate their position. At night, rotating searchlights identified Airways between cities. Navigation was by "Dead Reckoning" with only a compass, wristwatch and air speed indicator to confirm what you saw looking down at the ground.

On my return from Benton Harbor, having flown past all my "checkpoints" with surprisingly few cross-wind corrections, I didn't want this flight to end. No. If I had the fuel I would have continued flying. A foolish possibility, but for more than two hours I experienced the perfection and passion that so fulfilled and gave meaning to the life of Herbert W. Arnold, my first Flight Instructor who demonstrated that flying had another dimension. I now recognized the great gift he had given me and was grateful.

Before leaving for Pensacola for Basic, Instrument and Advanced Training I gave Lieutenant Dickey the traditional graduation "Thank You" present. A bottle of Bourbon. He turned away and put the package in his Locker pausing a moment to control his feelings.

Then, regaining his always stern professional composure, he thanked me. Shook my hand and said without a smile, "Take care, Norman. Don't get hurt. They need you out there."

Pensacola Naval Air Station is aptly called the "Annapolis of The Air". The Main Station's permanent red-brick buildings, mowed lawns, and surrounding Bays and Auxiliary fields were a welcome improvement over Bunker Hill's Army-style Barracks erected on a hundred acres of frozen Indiana farmland. Basic Training in formation and night flying at Ellyson Field in Vultee monoplanes with 450 horsepower engines began our carefully controlled transition to larger and faster combat aircraft.

Then, at Whiting Field, four weeks of Instrument flying in a 550 horsepower SNJ with retractable landing gear, resulted in not one embarrassing "wheels up" landing by forgetful Cadets. A notable achievement according to our relieved Instructors.

Then, at Bronson Field, adjacent to Escambia Bay, Advanced Training in Dive Bombing, low level Torpedo attacks, and Aerial Gunnery comprised an arduous curriculum taught by Flight Instructors working hard to keep over-eager Cadets from killing themselves. That there were few "Operational" accidents resulted from an attitude that Flight Safety was a habit acquired through constant disciplined drill. Instructors considered tough but fair were admired and there were many who truly cared about their "Boys" and earned our gratitude.

There was one exception. Marine Lieutenant Poor, otherwise known as "Piss Poor". Barely tall enough to meet the Naval Academy's minimum height requirement he was outraged by the sloppy appearance of Cadet's wearing oil-stained coveralls when not flying. The announced Uniform of the Day away from the Flight Line was washed ironed and starched Khakis, and that other Instructors were more casual about what Cadets wore merely stiffened Lieutenant Poor's resolve to impose Annapolis style discipline on high-flying Cadets.

My most savage dressing down was from Lieutenant Poor whose fury at my sweat-soaked and torn Flight Suit patched with a strip of adhesive tape surpassed a Marine Drill Instructor verbally abusing a recruit. He was incensed at my L.L. Bean Moccasins worn instead of heavy G.I. shoes more suitable for fighting in the Jungle than flying. My barely controlled anger was slightly mitigated when later I was told "Piss Poor" only beat-up on tall Cadets in revenge for his own lack of height.

Afternoons, far off-shore over the Gulf of Mexico, aerial gunnery practice consisted of flights of six Cadets attacking a fifty-foot long canvas target two hundred feet behind a fast moving tow plane. From a starting position off to one side and forty-five degrees ahead of the target, at timed intervals, each Cadet would in turn roll on to the target and fly a smooth "pursuit curve" hopefully placing a qualifying percentage of his color-coded bullets into the canvas sleeve. Concentration and smooth flying were essential to hitting the target.

A "Chase Plane" accompanied each flight to observe and later, after landing, score each Cadet's percentage of hits by counting the identifying colored paint smears on the canvas target. Most "Chase Pilots" were more than helpful. Their comments both in the air and on the ground explained what you were doing wrong and could immediately correct.

But not Lieutenant Poor. His high-pitched hysterical comments when we were flying shattered our concentration while attempting to hold the target in our gunsight. His constant screams of "Too high" or "Too wide" or "Too soon" compelled many Cadets to unplug their earphones.

One day returning to Pensacola from the Gulf of Mexico our Flight flew above a thick overcast that had been developing all afternoon. Lieutenant Poor, our "Chase Pilot", had ignored this weather change and now told us to continue on our present course while he descended under the clouds to determine our exact position. As on all our formation flights we passed the Lead from Cadet to Cadet on each new Leg or course change, and it was now my turn to be Flight Leader.

Ahead was the Gulf Coast of Florida. In an hour we would be over land. We had no word or sight of Lieutenant Poor. Our Flight continued flying North looking for a break in the clouds. Then after another thirty minutes, the unmistakable rotten egg odor of a Pulp Mill located our position over Flomaton, Alabama, fifty miles North of Pensacola. With fortunate timing an enormous hole opened in the clouds as our Flight descended under the overcast and, at an altitude of a thousand feet, followed the State Highway back to Pensacola.

Then, from high above the overcast we heard the familiar hysterical voice of Lieutenant Poor requesting our Flight's position. He repeated his frantic calls several times while by mutual and delighted agreement six Cadets remained silent simultaneously experiencing radio failure. Not an uncommon problem in old training planes.

When we were on the ground gathered around the canvas target scoring our paint-stained hits, our worried "Chase Pilot" landed and taxied over to us astonished, relieved, and grateful we were alive. He climbed out of his cockpit, hardly able to speak. "How?" he asked. "How did you get here?"

"Ask Norm," someone said. "He had the lead."
Lieutenant Poor suddenly remembered "beating up" on me. He looked sheepish. Shaking his head. "Magellan!" was all he said. "Magellan!"

When practicing "High Side" gunnery on a towed target, precise timing ensures that aircraft making separate runs at prescribed ninety second intervals do not collide. Exact intervals between planes prevents collisions among eager pilots concentrating on holding the target in their gun sight.

An attentive pilot carefully obeys the clock before winging over on to the target to estimate through his illuminated gunsight the angle, range, and "lead" required to score hits. Late one afternoon, fatigued after several hours in the air, one pilot misread his clock and flew his final run of the day out of sequence.

I was number three in that Flight and exactly ninety seconds after the plane ahead of me began its run, I rolled over on to the target concentrating my attention on flying a coordinated pursuit curve, breaking away, diving towards the sea and pulling out with as few "G's" as possible. Then I experienced the usual few seconds of total Blackout as I climbed to regain altitude, the blood slowly returning to my brain.

There, fifty feet in front of me I saw the out-of-sequence plane approaching head-on, its pilot seeing only the target, unaware of disaster. Semi-conscious, frozen in time, my vision cleared from black to gray as I watched and waited for the inevitable to happen.

Inexplicably, with no conscious decision by me, my hand shoved the control stick forward and in an instant the spinning propeller of the other plane passed over my head by no more than few feet. Stunned by what just occurred, I suddenly found myself all alone in an empty sky struggling to control a sharp stab of fear in my gut. After a few minutes, regaining full consciousness and self control, I "joined-up" on the other planes in my Flight returning to Pensacola.

I never reported this incident, nor learned if the other pilot ever discovered how close we were to killing each other.

Returning to Bronson Field, trying to concentrate on holding my position in the formation, I began to sing to no one but myself elated by an intense feeling that something mysterious and beautiful and unseen had saved my life and will always be there to help me make it through the years.

Looking back over my many years, I have always had a sense of someone or some power directing me, trying to tell me something, pushing me in one direction or another, illuminating my life.

Alone one night, flying over the sea I gazed at the hemisphere of stars rotating through the sky, while below, parallel rows of phosphorescent waves traced foam streaks formed by distant storms. Colliding Air Masses spinning around each other raised mountainous waves out of deep troughs traversed by a ship's wake, the stars, tracing orderly patterns in a constantly turning arc enveloped me with only the engine's roar, the dull, red glow of the instruments, the feel of the controls vibrating in my hand creating consciousness of time and place. All sense of here and now vanished for it seemed only the stars held my destination, the clock's second hand computing an Intercept Point far above the sea as I adjusted trim tabs, glancing at the instruments, looking far beyond familiar Constellations, I felt I flew formation on the Universe. My Wingman was Orion. And just ahead old Arcturus guided me in a giant arc to the Big Dipper.

I was part of this vastness as I studied the chart board, checked my Course Line and Fixes, the Time, Heading, and Speed connecting me to a moving Flight Deck somewhere below. Yes, the mystery of it all surpassed understanding and I wondered how to explain flying through the night above an indifferent sea? How does one tell about such things?

And yes. How does one tell about death?

What can ever mute the sound of a low-throated chattering propeller changing pitch in a black tropical night smelling of orange blossoms, salt air, and the feel of warm wind pressing a sweat-dampened Flight suit to trembling skin? Did I ever really think about death before? Removed from my world, one sweet smile, one voice now silent; those tap dancing feet will never jig across our Barracks floor; for he is ashes now, rather a smoke-blackened cinder hanging inverted from a bucket seat transformed into pure white dust of melted aluminum and magnesium. Pure white dust blanketed with fire-quelling foam that did not extinguish did not suffocate flames turning a delightful spirit into a memory. What the hell was his name? After all these years, what was his name? Who will remember anything but that he was always writing letters, forever reverberating shower stalls with high-pitched songs, words and melody surviving long after his death emerging from how many radios, how many record players, to evoke, in how many minds the thought that once I knew a guy who sang those words. Ridiculous songs. Sentimental lyrics. Yet, inexplicably, why should they retain such beauty, evoke such emotion?

The Landing Signal Officer frantically beat the air with fluorescent paddles, the "Talker" shouted into a deadened microphone, "one wheel down... one wheel down..." the Signalman aimed his Light gun, transmitting red flashes into the concentrated vision of a pilot focused on a perspective of hooded lights outlining two hundred feet of runway. "Wave-off!... Wave-off!... Wave-off!" screamed the "Talker", the LSO pleading "Come on son, get your head out of your ass..." the pilot throttling back, the aircraft settling, touching one wheel, one wingtip, its tail-hook failing to engage a restraining wire, digging a spinning prop into the macadam before cart wheeling into the darkness, the sound of ripping metal somehow triggering the high-pitched wail of a Crash Truck siren chasing a finger of flame into the night. A red Signal Rocket exploded overhead, closing the field now spreading a lake of flames, spectators crowding its shores, watching an asbestos clad Rescue Team swinging axes in the inferno, slashing at aluminum, prying back the crushed canopy, attempting to rescue the pilot cradled, head down in his shoulder straps, watching them struggle towards him with unseeing eyes, or was it a smile, one arm dangling in helpless greeting?

I restrained an impulse to raise my arm, to reply to that lifeless form disappearing in the flames. I stood there unable to move, wordlessly encouraging the spreading blanket of foam to choke the fire, allowing darkness to mercifully conceal death.

What was his name? After all these years, why
ask? Why remember? Why not forget? Why not
forget the memory of standing in the dark, throat dry,
clenching and unclenching my fists in helpless rage,
watching stumbling figures silhouetted against the
flames, jack-knifing the wreckage, gently lowering the
blackened corpse onto a canvas tarp that was folded
over how many times? Why remember the slow walk
to the Mess Hall, the green linoleum-covered tables
repellent in the fluorescent light, the Cooks standing
silently behind the food counter, for they had also
heard the siren, seen the flames, fed three times each
day, that wink, that grin, never failing to promote
a larger serving, a second helping, a boyish smile?
The young Pilots circled the table, sliding their food
trays, holding mugs of coffee to their lips, inhaling its
steam and the aroma of food, never once speaking of
death for before our eyes was an image of ourselves,
blackened bundles wrapped in canvas bouncing
in the rear of a pick-up truck, driving slowly to the
Morgue.

We thrust into our mouths servings of eggs and
steak and potatoes, fat chunks of bread vanishing as
if to compensate for the acquisition of knowledge
that would never vanish, never disappear, never
be drowned by the eating and drinking and other
pleasures of how many lifetimes?

GUATEMALA

Yes indeed. Words do belong to us all. Are common property. Create a sense of community. Shape history. Have dire and unexpected consequences.

John F. Kennedy's inaugural speech influenced a new generation stating we were - "Born in this century, tempered by war, disciplined by a hard and bitter peace, proud of our ancient heritage, willing to pay any price, bear any burden, meet any hardship, support any friend, oppose any foe to assure the survival and success of liberty."

Eloquent words proclaiming "The best and the brightest" of our nation would not merely react to events. They would make History happen.

Kennedy's speech inaugurated twenty-five increasingly aggressive years covertly de-stabilizing unfriendly governments. The CIA initiated and financed the replacement of seven democratically elected regimes with military dictatorships maintained in power by para-military death squads. The resultant fatalities and human rights violations were considered an acceptable price in defense of Western Civilization. After all, good honest men rationalized, did not massive collateral damage in Germany and Japan bring victory in the second World War.

Body Counts, Kill Ratios, and the total number of villages liberated, handed out to complacent Journalists at Saigon's Two o'clock Follies press briefings, measured the dubious probability of victory. These false expectations were contradicted by televised coverage showing the unrestrained destruction of a primitive peasant culture. Graphic scenes of human suffering aborted public support for a war that killed 58,000 Servicemen. After ten tragic years the light at the end of the Pentagon's rhetorical tunnel vanished.

As a writer and director of two TV films about the Vietnam War, I was a witness to a conflict that radically transformed our nation. The true cost of the fifty year Cold War greatly exceeded what Congressional budget estimates can ever account for. If we are to insure "Liberty for ourselves and our posterity," understanding the true price of containing communism is vital. For unexamined history will always be repeated, leaving future generations a bitter legacy of undesirable consequences.

Upon my return from California to New York in 1951 the motion picture division of the United States Information Agency was funded as an adjunct to The Voice of America. Under Directors Turner B. Shelton and Edward R. Murrow, their mission was to tell America's story, promoting understanding of our nation's essential values. As vital a task as any battlefield victory. A mission still unachieved. Criticism of American power, spreading from Europe to the Middle East, exacerbated by our support of Israel, some believe ultimately spawned the September 11th attack.

Anti-Americanism has a long history. In 1945 it was epidemic. Post-war European intellectuals, consistent apologists for Stalin's terror, opposed the cultural invasion of American films, books, and Coca-Cola bottling plants. Distinguished foreign Academics at European Universities established their liberal and progressive credentials by disdaining "ruthless American materialism, racism and economic exploitation." Their writings and lectures spread public ignorance of the United States, and when disseminated by the media, determined elections. Between 1945 and 1948 France and Italy's expanding Communist vote looked like the inevitable wave of the future. Europe seemed to be exchanging one totalitarian form of government for another no less destructive of human values.

To counter this trend, to achieve credibility, the USIA shunned propaganda. Adhering to un-sanitized truth soon won world-wide trust in USIA films and Voice of America radio programs. Adhering to BBC standards, the USIA became a reliable source of information about the world in which we live.

This was true of the more than fourteen USIA film scripts I researched and wrote. Only one, based on position papers and government briefings was based on disinformation, a questionable practice for a democratic government no matter how effective, no matter how high-minded the cause. To base Presidential findings and directives on fictitious success achieved through disinformation is to defy reality. Deal in illusions. Untruth becomes the foundation of government Policy. The seeds of our defeat in Vietnam were sown in Iran and Guatemala. The high cost of these first successful disinformation programs is with us today. Pre-emptive military action and Regime Change became US Policy with unintended consequences.

My first exposure to the Cold War was George Kennan's Foreign Affairs article advocating Containment. Immediately followed by Churchill's Iron Curtain speech dividing mankind into the ungodly East and the democratic West. A concept justifying the Truman Doctrine, the Marshall Plan, the Berlin Airlift and the formation of NATO. Far-sighted policies restoring hope to a world ravaged by the second world war.

In Greece, Turkey and Western Europe the communist vote declined. Threatened nations remained democratic. Berlin survived as a free city behind the Iron Curtain. And the rehabilitated European economy helped end America's post-war recession. Remarkable Foreign Policy achievements never surpassed by subsequent American administrations.

With the exception of the Bay of Pigs landing in Cuba, we employed a successful Cold War strategy using disinformation and the financing of military coups to oust emerging Leftist governments no matter how democratically elected. Regime Change, returning the Shah to power in Iran in 1953, was an intoxicating victory for American Strategists. They were reassured they could make history happen. Shape the future. Defend Freedom everywhere. No matter the cost.

Fifty years later my writing for the USIA evokes disturbing moral questions. Startled by recently revealed facts - I recognize in writing about - "Operation Success" - I didn't know much. And what I little I did know was wrong. In 1954 I was an unwitting purveyor of disinformation. A troubling thought when the tragic consequences of this disinformation can no longer be denied.

In June 1952, Jacobo Arbenz Guzman, the liberal democratically elected Guatemalan President redistributed to landless peasants 234,000 acres of a United Fruit Company's banana plantation. This Boston based corporation also owned Guatemala's rail and telephone lines and operated Puerto Barrios, the nation's major seaport. To reverse this appropriation, Sam "The Banana Man" Zemurray, United's owner, hired lobbyist Tommy Corcoran and Edward Bernays public relations firm.

Despite overthrowing a ruthless military dictatorship in 1950, and restoring democracy, President Arbenz, by legalizing Guatemala's Communist Party was perceived by our government to be a committed leftist with US ambassador John E Peurifoy reporting - "I am definitely convinced that if President Arbenz is not a communist he will certainly do until one comes along."

After a year of Sam Zamurray's anti-Arbenz PR and lobbying campaign, in August 1953, several days after replacing Mossadegh with the Shah of Iran, President Eisenhower authorized the CIA to remove Arbenz.

A propaganda campaign to discredit Arbenz emphasized his friendship with leftists. A political destabilization intensified by the threat of invasion by anti-Arbenz dissidents led by Colonel Carlos Castillo Armas, a graduate of Guatemala's Military Academy who had also studied at Fort Leavenworth, Kansas.

Financed by twenty million dollars and arms from the United Fruit Company, Armas' National Liberation Movement recruited 400 rebels and mercenaries and a squadron of ten surplus WWII fighters and transports flown by American freelance pilots. The clandestine radio "Voice of Liberation", broadcasting from Nicaragua, Honduras, the Dominican Republic and the US Embassy in Guatemala, evoked a constant expectation of imminent invasion.

Ignoring President Arbenz disclosure of CIA complicity, the American media accepted our government's denials. The presence of the "Soviet threat in America's backyard" was soon confirmed by the arrival of 2000 tons of Czechoslovakian rifles, artillery and land mines at Guatemala's Puerto Barrios. Enough weapons to convince President Eisenhower Communism had arrived on Central America's doorstep.

Exiled right-wing leader Carlos Castillio Armas with a hit list of 58 Guatemalan Communists, began a CIA supervised nerve war of death threats and assassinations, with false reports of massive rebel armies invading from Honduras and Nicaragua joined by thousands of volunteers. Operating from Honduran bases, rebel aircraft bombed the capital with leaflets demanding Arbenz surrender. Loudspeakers on the roof of the American Embassy accompanied puny rebel air attacks with greatly amplified sounds of massive explosions, evoking panic and convincing military leaders of inevitable rebel victory. After one government army refused to fight, the Chief of Staff asked for and received Arbenz resignation.

That month, United Fruit acquired its appropriated banana plantations. Castillo Armas outlawed all unions and political parties, creating a watch list of suspected communists and establishing a literacy test to disenfranchise peasant voters. President Eisenhower told a triumphant CIA "You have averted a Soviet beachhead in our hemisphere." A declaration confirmed by a documentary film of captured Czechslovakian small arms and munitions visually demonstrating Russian support of the Arbenz regime. 400 rebels equipped with fifty tons of American arms replayed the CIA's 1953 victory in Iran. An inexpensive triumph for Langley's geopolitical masters of disinformation.

Never anticipated was the unintended consequences of years of a brutal right-wing Castillio Armas dictatorship. A Civil War killing 200,000 civilians by Guatemala's military trained at the US "School of the Americas".

I do not agree with George Orwell working for the British Ministry of Information during the second World War who wrote: "All excursions into journalism, broadcasting, propaganda and writing for films, however grandiose, are doomed to disappointment." I was never disappointed. The success of USIA films was measured not in box office receipts but in official reactions to what we were revealing about life in the United States. Viewed at USIS Information Service Libraries in Eastern Europe, these films, books, and magazines were the only connection to the outside world for millions of citizens isolated behind the Iron Curtain. Unable to travel abroad, refusing to believe their own media, these audience risked careers and liberty to visit USIS libraries despite intimidating government surveillance recording each visit.

Electronic jamming of Voice of America, BBC, and Radio Free Europe did succeed in frustrating listeners hungry for accurate news from abroad. To thwart the increasing and devoted audience for USIA films, Iron Curtain regimes organized anti-American demonstrations often climaxed by government sponsored thugs setting fire to USIS Libraries.

There can be no greater compliment to writing's effectiveness than to evoke hysterical fear of the Truth. "Speaking Truth to Power" said Vlacav Havel, disagreeing with George Orwell, "is writing's ultimate mission." And with remarkably few exceptions, the USIA did, to the best of our ability, speak the Truth.

And what was this Truth? The popular *Ozark Project* portrayed the character and dignity of America's poorest, most rural, uneducated, region. *The School of the Ozarks* told of the restoration of hope and ambition through education of children moving out of a cycle of poverty and disease afflicting the area for generations. *Wilderness Library* told of a returning war veteran backpacking books to isolated families. A walking lending-library overcoming the illiteracy crippling the future of his neighbors children. *Ozark Newspaperwoman* told of eighty year old Maude Duncan producing a weekly newspaper in an effort to bring news of the "outside" into almost total rural isolation.

America. Warts and all. A stunning revelation to foreign audiences when contrasted with glamorous Hollywood representations of the United States.

The Man in The Middle told of a labor strike that did not occur in Stonington, CT. A dispute resolved not by extremists but by rational negotiators willing to compromise. *The Pursuit of Happiness* told of the freedom of choice of four unexceptional Americans struggling to support families, and have careers. *American Profiles*, produced in cooperation with NHK, Tokyo, told of six Japanese Americans becoming "Americanized" without rejecting their cultural traditions. *The Zelman Waxman Story* told of a Noble prize-winning Russian-Jewish immigrant who developed Streptomycin. The first effective antibiotic against TB. The documentary film *P.A.L.* portrayed an effective effort to cope with urban Juvenile Delinquency.

America in all its diversity. And judging by crowded USIS Libraries, attracting overseas audiences. Particularly, the film *Teaching English Naturally*. The first demonstration of the phonic method of instruction of our difficult language.

Telling the world that America had poverty, illiteracy, juvenile delinquency and labor management conflicts soon evoked rabid Congressional opposition. Not only was the USIA, at great expense to taxpayers, telling an undesirable message, the messengers themselves became suspect. Senator Joseph McCarthy began a notorious investigation of the USIA and State Department to expose "Left-wing liberals" and "Card-carrying Communists".

He conveniently ignored the fact Communist governments were burning down USIS Libraries showing these supposedly red-tainted American propaganda films. Senator McCarthy's cohorts, Cohen and Schine, toured USIA libraries to purge such literary classics as John Steinbecks *Grapes of Wrath*. Thornton Wilder's *Our Town* and mystery thrillers written by Dashell Hammet. An avowed "Red". Within a few years this hysteria burned itself out. But intelligent and effective USIA overseas information programs were irreparably damaged. The careers of outstanding State Department experts with invaluable knowledge of foreign areas were thwarted or destroyed. In the ongoing conflict between human intelligence and ignorance, ignorance prevailed.

It was also our misfortunate, acting on unwarranted assumptions, born of a successful disinformation strategy in Iran and Guatemala, that we participated in the Vietnamese Civil War not knowing what we did not know about that ancient civilization. America's Best and Brightest considered themselves Global Architects skilled at Regime Change in unfriendly countries through disinformation and assassination.

In 1961, "The Company", triumphant in Iran and Guatemala, convinced of their expertise as Kingmakers, unaware of what they did not know about the mood of the Cuban people, initiated the disastrous Bay of Pigs landing. A tragic failure due to ignorance, hubris and a misplaced faith in the effectiveness of disinformation attempting to call an invasion a liberation.

Playing the Game of Nations, changing regimes in the Congo, Indonesia, the Dominican Republic, Chile and Vietnam, our government ignored and frustrated the third world's desperate need for democratic reform.

Today, learning from our expensive Regime Change in Iraq, I hope we regain a decent respect for the Truth without which no problem of War or Peace can be solved.

Nothing enduring can be built upon a foundation of disinformation. I am encouraged when following the 9/11 attack the Pentagon aborted a plan to establish a Disinformation Office. Disinformation and our credibility as a nation can not co-exist. Abandoning our reliance on Truth, we surrender personal freedom in pursuit of the illusion of National Security. By our silence, by not protesting, we abdicate our independence as citizens during dark times when our government, skillfully exploiting the media, frightens a nation into submission. When "enhanced interrogation" and "alternative procedures" conceal the national degredation of torture, we lose what we are fighting to protect.

We must not remain silent before the desecration of the moral foundations of our country. When things fall apart, we can recover moral perspective by speaking the Truth to each other and the world. Words belong to us all. Are common property. Create a sense of community. Shape history. Have consequences. Words will keep us free.

PEEKSKILL

A descendent of two Presidents, Henry Adams observed in his 19th century autobiography - "Politics has always been the systematic organization of hatreds. And every society gives permission to hate."

Among all the hatreds distressing the world, certainly lynchings in America demonstrated the larger the mob, the greater the hatred, the more brutal the atrocity. A recent photographic exhibit of 100 years of our lawless executions shows otherwise peaceful citizens abandoning all ethical restraints. Ordinary Church-going Americans doing extraordinary Evil.

On August 27th, 1949, at Lakeland Acres picnic grounds near Peekskill, New York, several hundred American Patriots attacked the audience at Paul Robeson's fourth annual fund-raising concert benefiting the Civil Rights Congress, a legal defense group working for racial justice.

Preceding the attack local Public officials, the American Legion and other Veterans groups announced they would stage a patriotic demonstration peacefully picketing the concert. The local newspaper, the Evening Star encouraged them, proclaiming "the traitor and his followers not welcome" in Peekskill calling Robeson "violently and loudly pro-Russian. A black Stalin."

The Evening Star stoked further public outrage editorializing: "The time for tolerant silence that signifies approval is running out. Peekskill wants no rallies that support Iron Curtains... no matter how sweet the music."

By mid-summer 1949 popular war-time "Soviet-American Friendship" Committees were transformed by Cold War rhetoric into disloyal political fronts advancing communism. An exploding media feeding frenzy fed on news of a headline-grabbing Congressional Un-American Activities Committee jailing ten rich therefore unsympathetic Hollywood screenwriters as covert communists. More frightening were reports Nationalist China was about to be lost to the Red Tide now engulfing Asia. Disloyal Pinko's in the White House and State Department betrayed our "vital national interest" charged California's Senator Knowland, spokesman for Washington's China Lobby. Blacklists in the entertainment industry, and Loyalty Oaths for government employees, University professors, and high school teachers became acceptable national security procedures. Many Liberal Ministers and Priests, vigorous spokesmen for the disenfranchised poor, lost their pulpits. Liberal newscasters like Elmer Davis, now labeled Left Wing, lost their sponsors.

The voice of the Patriotic Right dominated the airwaves and shattered our national self-confidence. By 1949 being outside the mainstream of popular political thought destroyed careers. To be named a Parlor Pink, or Fellow Traveler, to have in the past contributed money or attended a meeting of one of the Attorney General's list of one hundred subversive organizations had disastrous career consequences. Unemployment, divorces and suicides were frequently the fate of anyone tainted Red.

This national hysteria even created a "Red Diaper Baby" category demonizing children of parents thought to be subversive. Yes. It was a time of civic madness exploited by politicians spouting dire warnings of the "Red Menace". A reliable vote-getter. An era one eloquent victim called "Scoundrel Time" when informers gave names of suspected communists to Congressional committees. To protect careers, friends denounced friends. The paranoid strain in American politics empowered alcoholic Senator Joe McCarthy to harass our State Department and intimidate Congress. Outraged by years of lies, with no proof of his accusations, the Senate finally censured their unscrupulous member for calling President Eisenhower and General Marshall communist dupes.

These allegations climaxed when Whitaker Chambers and Congressman Richard Nixon identified a high State Department official as a Soviet Agent. His presence at the Yalta Conference they insisted explained FDR's failure to prevent Russia's dominance of Eastern Europe. America's "Lunatic Fringe" also charged we were a nation betrayed by such distinguished Americans as Secretary of State Dean Acheson.

Public hysteria also resulted in an unfortunate dumbing-down of government decision-making. Knowledgeable multi-lingual scholars, students of foreign cultures remained silent or abandoned their vital advisory careers until political sanity was restored.

Our military and political leadership's abysmal ignorance of the historic Vietnamese conflict with China, and their tragic decision to intervene in a civil war resulted from the resignation or discharge from the State Department of loyal knowledgeable experts whose careers were destroyed during McCarthy's witch hunt.

Fighting an unnecessary war, 58000 servicemen paid a high price for our nation's flight into politically evoked hysteria.

In August 1949, when living in New Milford, preparing to move to California, I was not surprised reading newspaper reports of the Peekskill demonstrations. Picketing and violence seemed inevitable in a community where the influx of more affluent, better educated summer visitors were resented by local working class residents who thought classical music only for "Egg heads" and "Long Hairs". In neighborhood Bars, Blue Collar citizens drank and danced to the Governor of Texas singing on the Juke Box his popular vote-getting campaign song - "You are My Sunshine". Robeson's repertoire, several songs sung in Russian, seemed both a cultural and political affront to community taste.

What did hold my attention were reports that Paul Robeson never arrived at the concert. Blocked by a mob on the narrow road to the picnic grounds, he was rushed away to save his life. Paul Robeson?

A Minister's son. Rutgers first black All-American athlete. A Columbia Law School graduate unable to find employment as a lawyer who achieved immediate success on the concert stage, theater and movies. His great artistry brought world-wide fame. His baritone voice and performances in Shakespeare and O'Neill's plays stunned audiences with dramatic power. Truly an outstanding artist. An American success story. A role model for his race. I could not understand how Robeson became the target of an enraged mob shouting: "We're going to get Robeson. Lynch Robeson. Give us Robeson!" How was this possible, not in Mississippi, but in Peekskill, New York?

Paul Robeson, Langston Hughes, Richard Wright, and later Ralph Ellison and James Baldwin, were some of our most notable black artists and writers living in Europe. Free of America's racial tensions in London and Paris, they were highly celebrated and respected in societies where they felt accepted, their human dignity unquestioned. As expatriate Americans however, they became alienated, tragically unaware of the changing moods of their homeland.

Recording in England, and performing in all major European cities, Robeson lived in London and Moscow during the 1930's returning to the United States for stage or film appearances. Blind to the vicious racial prejudice prevalent in the Soviet Union, Robeson was an active apologist for Russia and the August 1939 Hitler Stalin agreement that initiated the second world war. Until the German invasion of Russia in June 1941, Robeson spoke at communist inspired Global Peace Conferences stating that men of good will "will not make war on anyone. Will not make war on the Soviet Union."

Paul Robeson was one of many peace advocates accepting Hitler's European conquests. Charles Lindbergh and other prominent Isolationists also agreed the war against Hitler was an economic and not a moral conflict but rather two tottering Capitalist

Empires, England and Germany, ruled by Bankers, fighting for financial supremacy.

In the United States, Robeson was falsely quoted saying "black Americans must never fight for the United States, a nation that oppressed them, against the Soviet Union, which treated blacks with fairness and dignity."

This misquotation was the most damaging of all his Soviet-friendly statements. When Germany invaded Russia, Robeson immediately called for the world to rise up and fight in defense of freedom, demonstrating that talented artists are not necessarily consistent thinkers. Then, during the Cold War, Paul Robeson resumed advocating peace abroad and racial justice at home to an America he did not understand.

He was unaware of the explosive volatile Cold War mood of the country. He did not understand the limitations of his fame. How few Americans recognized and celebrated his artistic and personal achievements. And how many rejected both his message and the messenger.

And tragically he was blind to demagogues exploiting television and the press to evoke unreasoning hysterical fear. Four years after defeating totalitarianism in Europe and Asia, Americans were advised to dig bomb shelters in their backyards, and train children to huddle under school desks. Once again America won a war and was about to lose the peace. People believed Russia would soon have The Bomb, if they had not already stolen its secret thanks to traitors like Robeson.

Ignorance, hysteria and television are a deadly combination. A great threat to our democratic institutions when wielded for partisan political purposes.

On August 27th the Lakeland picnic area contained only about a hundred pre-concert picnickers peacefully enjoying an early supper. About forty volunteers worked around the families to set up the concert stage and folding chairs.

Without warning a mob of 500 demonstrators rushed into the area throwing rocks, swinging clubs, and using fists to assault the picnicking men women and children and the working volunteers. Cursing the audience as "Commies and Jews", shouting "We're Hitler's Boys! We're going to get Robeson! Lynch Robeson! Give us Robeson!" the attackers were unrestrained by six local Policemen assigned to insure order at the concert.

Several phone calls to the State Police brought no protection despite repeated attacks by a mob threatening "no one will leave this picnic ground alive!"

The mob was a cross section of America. Out of control, otherwise decent citizens now enraged. As twilight faded, several crosses burned on nearby hills. An act attributed to mischievous teen-agers. Under a barrage of rocks and hand-to-hand fighting, the audience retreated to the bandstand as the hysterical mob ignited a huge bonfire of chairs and printed programs.

After two and one half hours of life-threatening assaults, the State Police arrived and the mob fled. In the parking lot, overturned cars and shattered windshields further demonstrated the mobs unreasoning violence. Miraculously no one was killed. Only thirteen people required medical attention.

Invited to again perform at Peekskill next Sunday, Robeson announced "From now on we take the offensive!... We'll have our meetings and our concerts all over these United States... I want my friends to know, in the South, in Mississippi, all over the United States, that I'll be there with my concerts. And I'll be in Peekskill too!"

Reading about Robeson's aborted Peekskill concert in the New York Times the following week evoked mixed feelings. Though I disagreed with his politics, I loved his music. And not just his Negro Spirituals. His *Ballad For Americans*, virtually unknown today, was a great musical dramatization of our history. And Robeson's performance of *Let My People Go* energized our nascent Civil Rights Movement. Despite his Communist sympathies, Robeson symbolized the promise of a better life for all Americans despite barriers of color and creed. Robeson was black, famous and rich. Unchained. Unbowed. And a threat to all fearing racial integration.

As Sunday, September 4th approached, I had second thoughts about attending the rescheduled Robeson concert. Peekskill was about an hour from New Milford. A pleasant afternoon drive. Perhaps my wife and I would have dinner on the way. Mojave, a trained singer and admirer of Robeson's voice, knew something about America that made her hesitate. As a school girl in El Monte California she watched Japanese classmates disappear into Relocation Camps. A heart-wrenching wartime experience that demonstrated the outrageous power of public hysteria. She was convinced further violence in Peekskill was inevitable. And she was right.

In June I had delivered my first film, *An Adventure in Friendship*, the story of four rehabilitated juvenile delinquents that was well received, and in August, having just completed a screenplay I anticipated driving West to try my luck as a free-lance writer-director. To go to the Robeson concert my last weekend in the East would mark a turning point in my life as well as an affirmation, a repudiation of mob rule. An intention I shared that evening with twenty-five thousand concert goers of all political persuasions. Left. Right. And middle-of-the-road they admired Robeson's singing and despised political and racial bigotry. As I drove Route 6 from Danbury to Brewster to Peekskill I was unaware of what was going on in Peekskill since August 27th. I saw none of the local bumper stickers reading "Wake Up America! - Peekskill Did!"

I knew nothing of the American Legion boasting "We run that Nigger Robeson out of town and would do it again!" The head of the Legion's Americanization Committee proudly announced "thirty thousand Patriots would march in a peaceful demonstration outside the concert." I knew nothing of these overt manifestations of vicious community hatred.

As I approached Peekskill I saw several hundred State Troopers assembled to control the crowd of two thousand demonstrators lining both sides of the highway leading to the concert grounds. To reach the Lakeland Acres Picnic Area the cars and buses ahead of me turned off Route #6 onto a black-topped narrow country road and slowed to walking speed. Studying the mile long line of stalled traffic I judged it would take at least an hour to reach the main entrance.

Patience has never been one of my virtues. The night was hot. My car without air conditioning. Moving ahead a few feet and then stopping to wait a few minutes before advancing again was frustrating. Thankfully, none of the other motorists relieved their frustration by horn blowing. Classical music lovers after all are Elitists. They shun vulgarity.

On either side of the road, New York State Troopers, directing traffic, and watching from under the brims of their campaign hats did not seem welcoming. Wearing dark glasses they appeared ominous, intimidating. Being called out to work on a hot Sunday was not their idea of good duty.

As we approached the main entrance, the increasing crowd of demonstrators on either side of the road began shouting at the slow moving cars. Vulgar racial and anti-semitic epithets.

However, as the line of cars moved slowly forward, responding to my undeniable anxiety and growing impatience, I made a U turn and abandoned my attempt to hear Robeson sing.

We stopped in Lake Mahopac for dinner untroubled by our failure to assert our constitutional right to peacefully assemble and hear music despite the tyranny of mob rule. We were also pleased to hear that evening on the car radio that Robeson performed undisturbed by the demonstrators outside the concert grounds.

Better safe than sorry, we returned to New Milford and a good night's sleep, unaware of what we would read in Monday's New York Times.

All the narrow roads leading from the concert were lined with demonstrators, many apparently drunk, bombarding the departing cars and buses with rocks and beer bottles. Flying glass from smashed windows and windshields quickly made the road slick with blood. Local families, some children as young as ten, were shouting and screaming and throwing rocks to express their hatred of fellow Americans who had been labeled "Jew Bastard Commies!" News photographs show fourteen year old girls standing beside policeman screaming and spitting at the fleeing Robeson fans. Incredibly some New York State Troopers, laughing at the rioting rock throwers, began searching departing cars "for hidden weapons", roughing-up drivers, throwing one to the ground, warning "Go back to Jew Town. If we ever catch you here again we'll kill you!" A frenzied State Trooper began beating cars as if to kill the vehicles with his nightstick.

Monday's Peekskill Evening Star saluted the Legion's Patriots joining the Mayor in blaming "the injured victims for coming to a community where they were not wanted."

The rest of the nation, fortunately did not agree. The prestigious Christian Science Monitor said the rioting followed "the Fascist pattern of violent suppression... the Klu Klux Klan pattern of Lynch Law." The New York Post called the Legion's Patriots "a mob of hoodlums run wild."

Despite the moral outrage expressed in newspaper editorials across the country, Robeson's American concert bookings declined precipitously while his overseas popularity soared. Peekskill and Robeson became symbols of American know-nothingism run rampant further sustaining Europe's left-wing anti-Americanism.

As an already declining blue collar Hudson River town, Peekskill struggled for the next twenty years to attract new industry, jobs, and educated middle class homeowners. Violence and public hysteria stoked by bigotry thwarted that community's future economic growth.

Twenty years later, Birmingham Alabama learned the same lesson after dispensing with Sheriff Bull Conner and his attack dogs. Mob rule can be very expensive.

In 1942, just prior to entering the Navy and Army, my college roommate Jack Helsell and I drove from New Hampshire to California. The trip was my initial discovery of America and during the war provided more than enough reassurance that what we were fighting for was indeed worth dying for. The America and Americans we encountered were open, generous, friendly, hospitable, and encouraging to youngsters about to report for military service. Jack to the Ski Troops and myself to Navy Flight Training. We discovered the America Frank Capra portrayed in movies. Good natured. Sentimental. And above all, trustworthy. America, outside the Cities, seemed in 1942 an endless series of small towns dramatized in Thornton Wilder's classic play *Our Town*.

In 3000 miles we saw no vulgar bumper stickers or ugly graffiti. Instead, delightful Burma Shave jingles marked the sides of roads that reached out to cross ever promising horizons. Arriving at San Francisco's glorious Golden Gate, with the entire span of the United States behind me, I understood for the first time Woody Guthrie's lyrics when he sang: "This Land is my land, this land is your land, this land is our land, this land belongs to you and me!"

Seven years later, driving the same California bound Route 66 with my wife, under the same "Big Sky" of the Southwest, post-war, Cold War America seemed to have changed in ways I did not like. Fearful heart-breaking changes. The Peekskill riot. Loyalty Oaths. Blacklisting. Political Witch Hunts by Congressional Committees appeared to be truly Un-American. The moral landscape of my beloved country had been altered with very few of my fellow citizens aware of what had been lost.

Supreme Court Justice Brandeis once observed: "Our government is the ultimate teacher of Good or Evil. Teaching by example. If our government breaks the Law, it breeds contempt for the Law, inviting every citizen to become a Law unto himself."

Today, in post 9/11 America, Attorney General Ashcroft in the name of National Security detains one thousand brown-skinned aliens and citizens without formal charges, indictments, or trial. With the President establishing Secret Military Tribunals to circumvent our legal system denying unnamed suspects the right to privately confer with a lawyer, I must ask what lesson is our government teaching? What are the long term consequences of our President breeding contempt for the Law in a society where so many parents teach their children to hate?

For the systematically organized hatred Henry Adams wrote about, which every society permits, lurks just under the surface of our violent culture waiting to be politically manipulated by leaders diverting public attention from their own misdeeds. Today, we are at war, until the body bags come home, wars unify a nation and focus public attention on victory. But what if in fighting terrorism there is no clear victory? No surrender ceremony? No ticker-tape parade down Fifth avenue? Can our democratic institutions survive ten more years of an endless struggle?

Yes. We survived Vietnam. Our second civil war. Following the turmoil of three political assassinations, and the savage human rights battles of the 1960's, the anti-war movement with all its domestic riots and bloodshed proved to be a working-out of the painful, often stumbling processes of American democracy.

Will this process occur again? Will we again be so lucky?

I am not without hope for the future. Our democracy did survive the grievous wounds inflicted by Vietnam, although the shrapnel that cannot be removed from our hearts will be with us always. Still, Pogo, the comic strip character was right when he said: "I have met the enemy, and he is us!"

PASCAGOULA

Ira Grimsley, five foot ten, 250 pounds of muscle
and fat tyrannized Pascagoula Mississippi wearing a
broad-brimmed Stetson hat and black cowboy boots.
A policeman known for his personal interpretation
of the law. A doctrine of violence inherited from
generations of Southern Officers and supported by
voters electing him Jackson County's Sheriff, he was
"The Man". A Law unto himself.

As a glorious sunset is unknown to the blind,
and Mozart's music unimaginable when deaf, I
knew nothing of the lawlessness practiced by Sheriff
Grimsley in communities where citizens were deprived
of legal rights because of race.

Although in 1955 TV broadcast grisly details
of the murder of black teen-ager Emett Till whose
only transgression was whistling at a white woman;
and later on Prime Time I witnessed the bloody riots
of Freedom Summer when Schwerner, Goodman
and Cheney were kidnapped, tortured and killed for
registering black voters; - televised tragedies seemed
distant and foreign, birth pains of a society violently

resisting change. Hopefully, precursors of a better future.

This belief in inevitable progress seemed confirmed in 1956 by my first direct experience of the South's racial cauldron while researching a film script in Montgomery, Alabama. Miss Rosa Parks, a courageous black house-worker jailed for refusing to sit in the back of the Bus inspired a year-long city-wide strike that bankrupted the Bus Company.

That black citizens agreed to walk rather than ride a segregated bus was no surprise. Miss Rosa Parks was a popular, courageous community leader defying white prejudice and hate. Walking to and from work every day evoked pride and asserted dignity in citizens compelled to drink from separate water fountains, eat standing at lunch counters, and use segregated toilets. Riding in the back of a bus was one more demeaning indignity. A daily insult Afro-Americans were now determined to resist.

Unexpected was the response of ordinary white citizens and worried downtown retail merchants. Needing servants and unable to survive financially without customers, housewives and the business community created and operated an alternative transportation system of station wagons and private cars driven by volunteers. The need for servants and customers prevailed over centuries of habitual discrimination.

At 31 I believed in rationality, confident that humanity's Better Angels ultimately will prevail over injustice. And in Montgomery in 1956 it appeared that personal convenience, economic need, morality and human conscience combined to bring about startling change. The Bus Company and City

Officials supported by the entire community reversed a humiliating practice in a culture where segregation was an integral part of the Southern way of life. Within a year Miss Rosa Parks rode in the front of a Montgomery Bus. The walls of hate separating blacks and whites seemed in that one Southern City, significantly weakened.

I was optimistic about the future of race relations. In 1954, in Brown vs. Board of Education, the Supreme Court ruled segregation unconstitutional. For supporters of Thurgood Marshall and Jack Greenberg of the NAACP Legal Defense Fund, lawyers arguing the case, the unexpected ruling was like winning the World Series. A remarkable achievement. Marshall's Brief describing the psychological damage segregation inflicts on schoolchildren was undeniable. Charles T. Duncan, a college classmate and friend, a Fund Lawyer, gave me a continuing commentary on the Legal arguments slowly moving through the Courts to ultimate success. A reassuring demonstration of the democratic process. An affirmation of the Rule of Law and the power of rational persuasion. The ultimate triumph of the Better Angels of human nature, a belief that sustained Abraham Lincoln during the Civil War.

In 1954, and again in 1956 in Montgomery, I did not foresee future race riots, burning black Ghettos, Churches bombed, schoolchildren murdered or attacked by police dogs and firehoses. In 1962, 30000 Federal Troops mobilized to enroll James Meridith in the University of Mississippi with a casualty count higher than the first Iraq war. Man's unrestrained inhumanity to Man seemed an endless tale of grief and strife.

In 1950, on location in Austin Texas, living in the Hotel Driskill, an elderly black Porter greeted me at the front door every evening when I returned at the end of a long day's work. He insisted on taking my camera equipment and tripods from my station wagon to my room. Frail. No more than five feet tall with fuzzy grey hair and an eager friendly smile, I feared the old man would have a heart attack carrying my heavy gear. Certainly a five dollar tip was insufficient payment for his life. He could not be dissuaded from this chore. Other Porters, respecting his determination, did not offer to help as he slowly trudged from the car to the elevator. Overloaded. Straining under the burden. And visibly proud he could compete with other younger men who called him "Pops". Arriving in my room, he would carefully stow the equipment in a closet, thank me for the tip and leave without another word. After several days of discomfort with his servile behavior, I understood "Pops" was not hostile or unfriendly but simply showing me he knew his place. Habitual obsequiousness. No familiarity. After several days of unhappiness about his downcast eyes, my curiosity and desire to be friendly intensified. I felt unjustly categorized as another bigoted white that blacks should fear. And being feared was a new and disturbing experience. A feeling of power over others I did not enjoy. An emotion not uncommon in the South where white men and women were usually considered life-threatening.

One evening, after a long hot day, as "Pops" stowed my gear in the closet, I removed two cold Coke bottles from the refrigerator and gave one to "Pops". He hesitated, nodded an embarrassed thank you, and turned to leave.

I said "wait a moment Pops" as I reached out and uncapped his bottle. "Pops" again turned and headed for the door as if eager to escape from this uncomfortable encounter.

I raised my Coke in a friendly greeting and took a long swallow. "Pops" looked down at his open bottle perplexed. Again he nodded thanks and confused, unable to respond, did not raise the bottle to drink with me.

"How are things Pops?" I asked. "How are you?"

The old man stared at me a moment. Shook his head. And could not speak.

"Been one long hot day," I said.

The old man nodded. Said nothing.

"I don't see how people can live here. Hot as hell!"

The old man just stood there. Surprised by my words.

Then he moaned, leaned over, held his head in his hands and began sobbing. Tears wetting his cheeks. I was stunned. Unable to say or do anything to comfort him. I felt foolish. Thought I said something stupid. Perhaps cruel. I offered "Pops" a chair and sat on the bed and for the next ten minutes watched the old man cry. An agony and grief I had never witnessed before. As intense and painful as the suffering seen on television every evening.

"Excuse me, Mr. Norman," Pops said, sobbing. "But I just buried my son. He was only 26."

"How did he die?" I asked.

The old man shook his head. Raised his eyes. A look of unbearable sorrow. No anger. No hatred. "They just killed him," he said. "They just up and killed him."

"Do you know why?"

"There is no why," he said. "There never is no why. Never."

The old man put the coke bottle on the table next to his chair and stood up. He turned to the door. "I must be going now, Mr. Norman."

"You haven't touched your drink."

"Thank you just the same, but best be going."

"Did you go to the Police?" I asked.

The old man paused in the doorway. Turned and stared at me.

"The Police?" he asked. "It wuz the Police what killed my son. Just beat up on him and threw him in the river and said he wuz drunk and disorderly. He wuz no drunk and disorderly my son wasn't. He wuz a Sergeant in the United States Army an decorated in the Battle of the Bulge and wuz home on leave just drinking with his friends in his uniform and all his decorations just as proud as a black man can be. Everyone wuz proud cause he wuz brave. Handsome. And when they pulled his body out of the river I couldn't look at what wuz done to my boy, Mr. Norman, I just couldn't look at his face and didn't want anyone to see him like that. You know, remember my son all beat up. Broken nose. No teeth. One eye gone. And then people tol' me I did wrong keeping the casket closed. They said everyone should see what wuz done to my boy. Everyone. But tell me, Mr. Norman. What good would that do?"

In 1962 Caravel Films sent me to direct a camera crew working in Pascagoula, Mississippi photographing the construction of the Grace Line's new luxury Cruise Ship at the Ingalls Shipyard. The first new American Ocean Liner to be built in more than twenty years. An historic event. The rebirth of American shipbuilding.

I remembered Pascagoula as a charming Gulf Coast town I travelled through on liberty weekends hitch-hiking from Pensacola to New Orleans during the war. Standing on the roadside in my immaculate dress white uniform and friendly smile, I never waited long for a ride usually accompanied by a free meal from patriotic citizens who would stop and lean out their car window and ask: "Where to son?" Their courtesy and genuine warmth never varied when told I was "a damn Yankee", and when I said Southern hospitality sure was different from New York, I became a most welcome guest.

Pascagoula's elegant pre-civil war mansions, cooled by gentle off-shore breezes and shaded by old Spanish Oaks, bordered wide avenues along a coastline of white sand beaches providing refuge for affluent upstate residents fleeing the heat and fevers of summertime Mississippi. This once handsome resort now "The Red-neck Riviera", entertains a different generation of vacationers today with unattractive cinder-block Motels, and miles of gaudy neon signs advertising Gambling Casinos.

In 1962, the gracious past was still visible. Pascagoula, where Henry Wadsworth Longfellow wrote *Evangeline*, the tale of Acadians the British Army removed from Canada to the Gulf Coast, memorialized his presence and the tragic history he dramatized. The beauty of the Old Inn we stayed at, and the graciousness of the friendly Staff created an atmosphere of civilized culture that one terrifying night proved to be a dangerous illusion.

Concealed behind a facade of graciousness lurked bigoted White Citizens Councils. Respectable church-going middle class businessmen who accepted blue-collar Klu Klux Klan violence as a legitimate defense of Southern society. A Guarantor of White Supremacy. That inhumanity, brutality, murder and racial hatred were essential to protect the Southern way of life was rarely challenged by the overwhelming majority of white citizens. Presiding over this closed society, ensuring conformity to the True Faith of the Southern States were the elected County Sheriffs who theoretically could be removed from office only by a higher civil authority.

Not subject to any administrative review or sanction, the unrestrained lawlessness permitted by County Sheriffs made Vigilante bombings of homes and churches and brutal murders and lynchings acceptable behavior for generations of southerners. Killing blacks with impunity was no crime. No aberration.

Pascagoula was a Police State where Sheriff Ira Grimsley's concept of The Law prevailed. The so-called "Pope of Pascagoula" ruled by fear, organizing and training his own strong arm squad of Storm Troopers called the "Jackson County Citizens Emergency Unit", determined to eradicate local "nigger lovers"; boycott dissenting businessmen who curry favor with black customers by calling them Mr. or Mrs., and informing the Missippi State Sovereignty Commission of Segregationists who were to be vilified, threatened, and boycotted.

Heading this secret list of undesirable citizens who thought and wrote about blacks as human beings were Southern Journalists like Pulizer Prize winner

Ira B. Harkey, Jr. of Pascagoula, and Hodding Carter II of Grenville. Heroic editors who survived threats to their lives and boycotting by intimidated advertisers.

All other journalists, particularly News cameraman and photographers from "up North" were not welcomed by the ruffians and thugs seeking to protect their sanctified image of the South. A romantic vision their violent and often drunken behavior defiled. Though unaware of it, our production crew from New York were considered troublemakers, another Yankee intrusion stirring up "nigras" who are perfectly happy when left in their place. Scenes of police brutality on national TV and in Life magazine outraged southern pride. The South couldn't stand seeing themselves as others saw them. Sadistic Goons. Backward. Ignorant. Bigoted Rednecks. Certainly not the elegant aristocrats portrayed in *Gone With The Wind*.

Smashing cameras and intimidating journalists was the mindless response of outraged Vigilantes. Some Television journalists asked for "Combat Pay" when sent South.

The desk clerk was absolutely charming recommending an old ante bellum mansion converted to a southern style restaurant located about ten miles from Pascagoula. We would enjoy a traditional meal served with graciousness and elegance, a reminder of the vanished culture of the "Old South".

That evening, accompanied by my cameraman and unit manager, I drove out of town on an old state highway through a landscape of magically changing colors as the setting sun slowly transformed twilight into the mysteries of a southern night. I was driving through and seeing William Faulkner's Mississippi for the first time, truly understanding his passion for a bountiful land of cotton fields and Pecan groves. I recalled another southerner, Horton Foote, and his play *A Trip To Bountiful* and felt some of his yearning for a bountiful past being obliterated by unrelenting "progress".

The air we breathed seemed soft and gentle. Perfumed by lilac and the pungent odor of recently plowed black topsoil. Drained by our long day's work, we were silent driving along that highway, staring out the window, anticipating a good meal, a restful sleep and another day working under a hot Mississippi sun. We enjoyed being where we were, enthralled by a scenic beauty that could not be denied.

Glancing into the rear view mirror I noticed a car's headlights maintaining its distance behind me. Observing the posted speed limits, driving no more than fifty miles an hour on a flat straight highway, it seemed strange this other car did not overtake us. Slowing down, the interval between cars did not change. The size and shape of the headlights reflected in the mirror did not vary when I accelerated. We were being followed. Tailed. Pursued. And it was not a State Trooper with identifying rooftop lights. I said nothing to my passengers who were half-asleep.

A scene out of a "Counter-Spy" script I had written years before. Harding, my hero, driving a lonely country road at night narrowly escaped his pursuers in a hair-raising chase that tonight, on this Mississippi highway, was real. I felt the familiar dry taste of fear. Heart pumping. Adrenaline flowing. Was I just over-reacting? Had recent shocking headlines about the south combined with fatigue and imagination to evoke paranoia?

Following the Desk Clerk's precise directions I turned onto a narrow black-topped country road leading to the restaurant. In the mirror I was not surprised to see the following car come off the Highway and maintain the interval between us. I speeded up, driving towards the lights of the old Mansion in the woods less than a mile ahead. Then, as if following an old script, I pulled off on the shoulder of the road, stopped and turned off my lights. When the pursuing car roared past I U-turned onto the road and raced back on the highway to Pascagoula.

From the back seat a frenzied voice shouted: "What the hell are you doing?" And beside me, the cameraman screamed, "Turn on your headlights before you kill us!" I floorboarded the accelerator doing over a hundred miles an hour. In the mirror the headlights raced after us growing bigger every mile. My passengers turned and looked behind. There was nothing more to say. Our danger was real, not make-believe.

Flying taught me control of unreasoned fright. Gut-wrenching fear. Panic threatening my mind. Such dark ordeals of body and soul now turned me cold. I concentrated on driving. Working hard to save our lives.

Pascagoula's narrow streets slowed us down with our pursuer less than a hundred yards behind. Then we heard what sounded like an engine back-firing. Once, twice, three times. Loud and clear. "Jesus Christ!" the cameraman screamed, "They're shooting at us!" as both rear tires blew out and I continued driving on bare metal rims, the chase finally ending at the Sheriff's Office as the other car, a black four door sedan occupied by several men raced by its horn blaring triumphantly.

We ran into the building and met Sheriff Ira Grimsley standing in the doorway. The metallic screech of wheel rims rolling on the pavement, engines racing, and horns blowing lured him from his chair behind his desk to ask: "What in God's name going on out here?"

As unattractive in person as he was in his Life magazine photograph, Grimsley was defiantly overweight, had a flushed drinker's face, and wore a sloppy stained Confederate grey uniform, a caricature of a dangerous uncouth back-slapping joke-telling southern Lawman.

Unable to speak we were still frozen in fear. "Who was driving that damn car?" Grimsley asked.

I nodded. "Should arrest you for disturbing the Peace," he said angrily. "Don't you know better than driving 'round like that? Chewing up good tires. Making a Hell of a racket!"

I attempted to explain. Told him of the high-speed chase. The gunshots. The punctured tires. "What the hell you expect?" he shouted. "Driving that fast. Tires overheating. There's not a tire wouldn't blow at that speed. Lucky you weren't all killed."

I agreed. "Damn lucky," I replied, describing the black four door sedan and gun-toting Rednecks shooting our tires. "Rednecks Hell!" he shouted. "What do you mean Rednecks? And what do you mean shooting?"

I insisted there were gunshots. Rednecks.

He shook his head. Pointed a fat stubby finger at our car. "Sounded more like a clapped out engine backfiring."

Again I insisted. "They tried to kill us."

Sheriff Ira Grimsley threw back his head and laughed. A full throated belly laugh. His fleshy jowls jiggled. "God damn it to hell," he said. "The most happened was a bunch of Good Old Boys having a little fun. If they intended to do you hurt believe me you wouldn't be standing here right now telling me your cock and bull story. Believe me. No way."

Returning to the Inn, still shaken, unable to sleep after draining a bottle of Johnny Walker Scotch, we all agreed we got the message. Tonight's nightmare was a warning. It would be stupid to remain in Pascagoula to find out what was going to happen next.

This was Sheriff Grimsley's town and these Good Old Boys were his boys. His messengers.

I phoned Cal McKean my Caravel Films Producer at his home apologizing for the late Call. Cal sounded relieved to hear from me. "I've been phoning you all evening ," he said.

"We went out to dinner."

"That's what I thought," Cal said. "I've been trying to reach you."

"What's the problem?"

"I want you to come home," Cal said. "Right away."

"We haven't finished the script," I explained.

"We'll use what you got. Wrap up and get the hell out of there."

"O.K." I replied. "We'll leave tomorrow. We've had it with this town."

147

"From what I saw on television tonight all Hell's broken loose," Cal said. "Rednecks burning buses and breaking heads and they just killed a Minister praying for a crowd of demonstrators kneeling on the steps of a Courthouse."

"Anything else?" I asked.

"Yes," Cal said, anxiously. "A CBS Cameraman got beaten up real bad. Camera smashed. Car overturned and burned. He's in a hospital with a fractured skull."

"I hear you Cal," I said. "I hear you. We'll be home tomorrow night. Thanks for the call."

PREVENTIVE DETENTION

On Sunday, May 2nd 1971, "Tora Tora Tora", the Japanese code words initiating the Pearl Harbor attack, transmitted at 6:10 A.M. by Police Chief Jerry Wilson, ordered 14,000 District Police, Army, Marine and National Guardsmen into Washington's West Potomac Park to evict 50,000 Peace marchers. Thus began another day in American history that will also live in infamy.

Helicopters offloading a Marine Battalion at the Washington Monument asserted the government's determination to end 15 days of anti-war demonstrations that included disabled veterans discarding medals on the Capitol steps. Following Saturday night's Rock concert, the Attorney General, without prior notice, revoked the demonstrators camping permits and ordered the preventive detention of 13,400 Americans. The presumption of innocence, a historic legal protection against false arrest and conviction, was replaced by the presumption of guilt. Ignoring their Constitutional right to bail and due process, law-abiding citizens were arrested for predicted rather than actual behavior. Our government acted

149

on the basis of accusation, when no crime had been proven, and when no crime had been committed. A Justice department spokesman justified this illegality insisting "our national existence was at stake," and the Federal government "had a right to do whatever was necessary to keep this city open."

The Department of Justice then issued a list of anticipated terrorist threats. Hard intelligence from reliable sources predicted bombs destroying Potomac bridges, balloons suspending wires to entrap Helicopters, and the discovery of hidden caches of dynamite, helium tanks, and plastique explosives. Attorney General Mitchell watching the demonstrators, compared the Peace activists to the Bolshevik revolutionaries of 1917. "A threat that must be met with a massive show of government power."

At the District of Columbia's Command Center, Mayor Walter Washington and his staff had a different appreciation of this "March on Washington". They were confident they could maintain the Capitol's record of peacefully coping with massive demonstrations. In 1963,1968,1969, and 1970, as many as 800,000 demonstrators marched down Pennsylvania avenue peacefully gathering at the Washington Monument to assert their right to petition their government.

For more than a year I had been researching a documentary on civic unrest. The assassinations of JFK, Robert Kennedy and Martin Luther King, and the Civil Rights and anti-war protests of 1968, 1969 and 1970 were extraordinary events studied by two Presidential Commissions issuing reports that did not convey the human drama involved.

When the Commissioner of Public Safety, Charles T. Duncan invited me to observe the District's

Command Center at work, I flew to Washington welcoming an opportunity to witness the decisions of Officials responsible for maintaining order in a large American city. I believed Mayor Walter Washington had achieved a proper balance between demonstrator's rights and the laws he had sworn to uphold. A role model for other cities coping with mass demonstrations. I soon found the Mayor was a powerless observer of events, merely observing the decisions of Police Chief Jerry Wilson who followed Attorney General Mitchell's illegal orders.

Based on the fallacious concept of Qualified Martial Law, the Department of Justice bypassed the District Government's authority acting as if valid Martial Law existed without the findings required for a Presidential Proclamation. Without a Proclamation, the District government would be responsible for the illegal acts of the Federal government.

Controlled by the Department of Justice, the District Police suspended the use of Field Arrest Forms establishing Free Arrest Zones, arresting everyone in designated areas of the city. Without properly executed Field Arrest Forms, the Police made arrests that could never be prosecuted. "Just load 'em up! And lock 'em up!" Attorney General Mitchell and Assistant Attorney General Kleindienst announced. For John Wilcox walking in a Free Arrest Zone at the Washington Monument, these comments, transmitted on police radios, soon found him writhing on the sidewalk, his kneecap shattered by a police baton.

According to Fred Wilcox's sworn Affidavit, one of a thousand filed in successful litigations resulting from police actions, an officer emerged from a patrol car brandishing a baton. As Wilcox shouted "Non violence! Non violence!" he was clubbed across his knees and fell to the ground. "Get the fuck up" the officer screamed. "It's time for me to kill you." Ignoring Wilcox's pleas "I surrender. I give up," the policeman pounded Wilcox's head, ribs, knees and shins shouting "Get the fuck up! Get the fuck up!"

As detainees were swept into Detention Centers, a Department of Justice press release stated "This use of Qualified Martial Law kept the city open for business without injuring anyone. Police behavior was exemplary. A role model for other cities." The media published this disinformation describing Police "forbearance, skill and restraint."

Sworn Affidavits of 178 witnesses told of 231 incidents of excessive force, 58 involving the use of batons or fists, contradicting the government's statement "no one was hurt." Other Affidavits described unmarked police cars charging into crowds as Officers removed their name tags before spraying tear gas and mace, threatening to throw handcuffed demonstrators into the Potomac, screaming "let's make it so they can't walk anymore!"

Several Governors and Mayors, and President Nixon congratulated Police Chief Wilson who assumed responsibility for these tactics. Life magazine praised him "for his decisive demonstration of Law and Order." And protected by media disinformation, the Attorney General evaded his personal accountability.

The most serious flaw in this deception was an incredible oversight. Where do you feed and shelter 13,400 detainees for four days? Without Field Arrest Forms how do you assemble accurate arrest records with fingerprints and photographs? How then do you legally free detainees without creating judicial chaos?

ACLU Director Aryett Neir called the Department of Justice's procedures "a planned process of perjury" with seven arresting officers, signing their names in rotation, falsifying arrest records.

With a processing rate of 60 detainees an hour, many ill or injured, fingerprinting and photographing the first day's sweep arrests of 7200 demonstrators foundered.

I visited several Detention Centers. At the Central Lock-up, demonstrators were confined for more than forty hours in cells six feet square. Without ventilation or space to lay down, unfed for eleven hours, with inoperable toilets, denied medical attention, the Detainees were physically assaulted or threatened. "You're gonna be raped in here!" Guards shouted. "We're gonna put you in cells with murderers!" sworn Affidavits cited.

At the Coliseum I saw 3,000 demonstrators attempting to sleep without blankets on a cold concrete floor. Denied food or water for ten hours, with malfunctioning toilets, and with the prospect of another 24 to 48 hours detention, many accepted a disorderly charge and arrest record posting a $10 collateral despite being guilty only of walking through a Free Arrest Zone.

At the Third Precinct Jail I saw demonstrators who were maced in their cells. One cell had been drenched by police water hoses and threatened with Tear gas if demonstrators didn't stop singing *We Shall Overcome*.

U.S. Superior Court Judge James Belson visiting the Central Lock Up reported to the D.C. Public Health Association that "600 persons now detained prior to arraignment ... are being held under conditions which grossly violate minimum standards... the petitioners are experiencing cruel and unusual punishment and irreparable injury by reason of being held in the detention facility described above."

On Tuesday May 4th, at 1:30 P.M., demonstrators at the Department of Justice building were unaware that eight empty school buses and 120 Policemen in riot gear were converging on them. Following orders to "Lock everyone up" the Police released Tear Gas, and without first announcing orders to disperse, charged into the crowd swinging clubs, using Mace, punching and then dragging demonstrators to the buses parked nearby.

At 2:47 P.M. after 77 minutes of unrestrained police violence, an Armored car appeared ordering the demonstrators to disperse or be arrested. "This is an unlawful assembly" was repeated several times as demonstrators, enclosed within surrounding barricades attempted to flee.

On Wednesday May 5th, at 3:28 P.M., as Congressman Charles Rangel addressed demonstrators on the Capitol steps, the Police cordoned-off the area and arrested 1200 American citizens assembled to protest Official Lawlessness.

"We'll worry about the Constitution later" said Deputy Attorney General Richard Kleindienst justifying the Justice Department's illegal actions.

That evening, returning to the Command Center I learned the Courts were dismissing all cases brought before it, unfairly castigating District Officials for the massive illegality of sweep arrests, and protesting the abuse of their already overloaded Court Calendars.

In 1968 I witnessed several riots evoked by the Martin Luther King assassination. I had also

seen and photographed the burned-out ghettos of
Newark, Detroit and Washington. Events that seemed
historically inevitable. In August 1965, while working
on a film in Los Angeles, I walked the arson devastated
streets of Watts after a six day riot that left 34 dead and
1000 injured. Sparked by a mishandled police traffic
stop, the destruction appeared spontaneous, evoked by
intractable despair and injustice. There was nothing
organized or controlled about the random burning
of buildings or festive looting or violence initiated by
unrestrained human rage. "It just happened," said the
Los Angeles Mayor. "A mindless tragic event."

The May 1971 cold-blooded, deliberately
intimidating, pre-planned and skillfully implemented
response of the department of Justice to peaceful
protest was different. And more troubling. What I
witnessed for four days shocked me more profoundly
than the other violent incidents. Fundamental
constitutional rights were violated by a calculated
government decision. All I had been taught and
believed since my first civics class had been rejected
by the U.S. Attorney General ignoring what King
John established when signing Magna Carta in 1215.
The subordination of authority to the rule of law.
Abrogating the ancient right of petition and all that
flowed from it was unacceptable, intolerable, though
not unprecedented in our history.

TV and newsphoto images, transmitted
nationally, shocked and shamed readers previously
unsympathetic to anti-war demonstrators. The
overcrowding, lack of food, water and adequate
sanitation, the pictures of law-abiding citizens, some
ill from Tear Gas or Mace, shivering in unheated cells
seemed un-American.

Nevertheless three weeks later, a national poll found 76% approved of the government's actions. A New York Times editorial stated "If political tyranny ever comes to America, it is likely to arrive as a uniquely American way of preserving this country's traditional values. Instead of tyranny being the dramatic culmination of radical protest and revolution, it can come silently, slowly, like fog creeping in on 'little cat feet'."

What is happening to my beloved country? I wondered then, and wonder now, recalling these events amidst today's paranoid concentration on National Security. Has our government's disdain for the rule of law moved our nation down the slippery slope of lawlessness justifying preventive detention? All national polls indicate a majority of Americans approve of preventive detention as a response to terrorism.

And illegal immigration.

Our heartless detention of immigrants without visas certainly contributed to the international legal and moral disgrace of Guantanamo Bay and Abu Ghraib. Preventive detention has become as "American as apple pie".

Seven years after the 1980 Mariel "Boatlift", in 1987, 3800 Cuban refugees remained in indefinite detention - one immigrant fleeing Castro's tyranny, judged a danger to society, was detained for 11 years. In 2004, the Supreme Court freed the remaining 750 Mariel detainees ruling the government's use of indefinite detention illegal. A decision faithful to our nation's sense of morality, an outrage still being challenged by the department of justice.

Why do we justify and accept mistreatment of immigrants and enemy combatants? Why, since 9/11, do we refuse to acknowledge the fear-driven changes in what is acceptable government behavior in a democratic society?

I believe these changes are the consequences of the illegal arrests I witnessed in 1971 in Washington's Free Arrest Zones when 13,800 Americans were swept into preventive detention with the approval of 76% of their fellow citizens. By condoning this flagrant violation of inalienable rights, an essential foundation of our national character was undermined. Our once cherished and respected government under Law changed. Perhaps forever. The self-correcting political dynamics of our democracy aborted with the majority of American voters preferring self-congratulatory myths and deceptions to self-evident facts. The basis of all Law.

These troubling changes can be explained by a history embodying the narrative of our nation's development telling us what it has been, and most important what it is to become.

On March 31, 1942, the Justice Department issued the shameful "Civilian Exclusion Order" directed at 125,000 Japanese residents, 70% of them American citizens. Given between three days and two weeks notice of their compulsory detention, transferred to 13 barbed-wire Relocation Centers in seven states, these loyal citizens lost their homes, farms, businesses, and tragically, their freedom. Aroused by false evidence of military necessity, columnist Westbrook Pegler stoked "Jap" hysteria stating "the Japanese in California should be under armed guard to the last man and woman right now, and to hell with habeas corpus until the danger is over." A high government official agreed and responded by advising shooting on sight all Japanese residents of California. A Los Angeles Times editorial then stated: "A Viper is nonetheless a Viper wherever the egg is hatched. So a Japanese American born of Japanese parents grows up to be a Japanese and not an American."

Los Angeles District Attorney Dockweiler added to this hysteria warning - "it was time for the people of California to disregard the law to secure their protection."

The entire California Congressional delegation passed a resolution insisting on "the immediate evacuation of all persons of Japanese lineage and all others, alien and citizen alike, whose presence shall be deemed dangerous or inimical to the defense of the United States." The American Legion issued a resolution stating "that it wasn't enough to keep ethnic Japanese in concentration camps - they should be deported." .

General John L. DeWitt, the Army commander ordering relocations, called Japanese American citizens "non aliens" declaring "There isn't such a thing as a loyal Japanese, and it's just impossible to determine their loyalty by investigation."

On the night of February 24th, 1941, public hysteria made inevitable the comic "Battle of Los Angeles" when Army radar reported an attack by non-existent Japanese airplanes. Anti-aircraft batteries exploded 1400 3 inch shells over the city with falling shell fragments damaging only automobiles and rooftops.

The War Relocation Authority directed by Milton Eisenhower with a budget of eighty million dollars, was established to house and feed detainees in what was inaccurately described as our country's first National Defense Migration.

A deliberate misreading of American history.

In 1838, defying a Supreme Court ruling, President Andrew Jackson enforced the Federal Indian Removal Act ordering the Army to move the entire Cherokee Nation along the Trail of Tears, from their prosperous Georgia farms to preventive detention on barren Oklahoma prairie reservations.

Attorney General Anthony Biddle, conscious of this historic precedent, vigorously opposing his administration's illegal decisions observed - "that the present practice of keeping loyal American citizens in concentration camps for longer than necessary is dangerous and repugnant to the principals of our government."

Another outspoken Cabinet member protested. Secretary of the Interior Harold Ickes, outraged at the violation of citizen's rights wrote President Roosevelt insisting "the continued detention of these innocent people in relocation centers would be a blot on the history of this country."

Sixty years later, preventive detention is now used as an effective method of controlling dissent and preventing political opponents from challenging authority. Denying parade permits to activists, cordoning off political candidates with Secret Service checkpoints and police barricades are now accepted by the media and public as vital security measures. In August 2004, the city of New York, in contempt of a court order, shielded Republican convention delegates from anti-Bush demonstrators by arresting and then jailing 1806 protestors beyond the required 24 hour limit between arrest and arraignment. The majority were not freed until the convention adjourned.

Preventive detention must not be allowed to displace a legal concept that truly reflects who and what we are as a nation. Our historic presumption of innocence must once again prevail as the foundation of the rule of law.

Which then evokes the question: - what constitutes The Rule of Law? Are all laws necessarily legal?

In 1933 legally elected Nazis Leaders immediately erased the distinction between a political party and the German state. They became inseparable, one and the same, with all the horrors of Hitler's regime judged legal by a judiciary serving a criminal government.

For 12 years, under Nazi German law, torture of declared "enemies of the state" was justified by Werner Best, the nation's chief legal counsel ruling: - "so long as the police force carries out the will of the country's leadership, it acts legally."

In 2003, Alberto Gonzales, our nation's chief legal counsel justified the government's use of torture stating "that the President has the power to order any measure pursuant to his core authority as commander in chief." Jay S. Bybee, the conscience of the Justice Department as head of the Office of Legal Counsel in another memorandum ruled: - "As Commander in Chief the president has the constitutional authority to order interrogation of enemy combatants. Acting under his inherent powers as commander in chief, the president can lawfully order torture without regard to federal criminal laws or international laws. Any measure that interferes with the president's direction of such core war matters as the detention and interrogation of enemy combatants would thus be unconstitutional. Even Congress lacks the power to limit presidential prerogatives."

Today, presidential prerogatives include the disappearance of enemy combatants of high value to interrogators in foreign locations. Held at Top Secret sites in violation of international law, an unknown number of ghost detainees are concealed from surveillance by the International Red Cross and their governments.

Why are we silent? Why do we not protest? Magna Carta, the Bill of Rights, and the Constitution have not been repealed or annulled. Our refusal to protest the loss of our rights and our support of preventive war are moral failures.

Lacking moral courage, we are forgetting our history of defending "Life, Liberty and the pursuit of Happiness." A source of pride and national honor. Fortunately we have also been inspired by leaders who appealed, in Lincoln's words "to the better Angels of our nature." Hopefully they will arise again to save us from our cowardice. Our complacency. Our self-deceptions. Our patriotic fantasies.

Today, driven by fear, our historic devotion to the rule of law has been diminished by lesser men who divert our attention from violations of our most fundamental freedoms. On Inauguration Day, President George W. Bush asked our nation "to spread liberty abroad" while ignoring the sacrifice of our liberty at home in an endless war on terrorism.

A bad exchange. A bad bargain.

As Benjamin Franklin said: - "They who would give up an essential liberty for temporary security deserves neither liberty or security."

CHARLIE

Like it or not, dining in Dartmouth's Thayer Hall was compulsory for Freshmen. In a large and austere room 800 students, stoking ravenous appetites three times a day, socialized with their classmates and often initiated lifetime friendships. Although Thayer's cafeteria style menus lacked the variety and taste of Hanover's more appetizing restaurants, most students accepted without dispute this surrender of dietary freedom.

An unforgettable memory. Standing in the serving queue, quelling hunger pangs, impatiently moving past steaming food cauldrons before exiting into a large dining hall crowded with rows of long tables. After filling our trays, we then searched for and found unoccupied seats, rarely sitting down with the same students twice. With time, and familiarity, however, human nature being inexorable, regular dining groups formed. Dormitory neighbors and roommates, public high school or prep school classmates, and athletic teammates, often gravitated together in a voluntary process described in Sociology textbooks as "Bonding".

Our crowded mid-day meals reverberated at the decibel level of a Boiler factory, clattering food trays, raucous laughter, and high-spirited voices greeted late arrivals compelled to search for and occupy tables at the far end of the hall. One memorable day, emerging from the serving line, balancing a tray in one hand, hot coffee in the other, I looked for and located a vacant seat. There, as if waiting for me at the far side wall, under a window looking out over the campus, I found a table occupied by a solitary student. Carefully crossing the Hall, without spilling my coffee, I sat down, extended my hand, and introduced myself. I was greeted with a broad charming smile, a nod, and from a mouth now occupied with food, not a word of welcome.

Thus began an enduring friendship of sixty-two years.

Charles Duncan, I soon learned, was the son of Todd Duncan, the original Porgy in Gershwin's *Porgy and Bess*. One of my favorite Operas. Raised in the District of Columbia where his father chaired Howard University's Music department when not performing on stage or screen, or concertizing in Europe, Charlie's early childhood included several months a year living in luxury Hotels and crossing the Atlantic in ocean liners while thriving on the love of adoring parents.

The Northfield Academy, a Prep school in Greenfield Massachusetts, provided Charlie's other home where he enjoyed happy teen-age years of high academic achievement, personal popularity, and above all, learning to ski.

A shared passion. The topic of our first conversation.

In 1940, Stowe Vermont's Mt. Mansfield installed New England's first Chair Lift, a great improvement over arm-wrenching rope tows. I impressed Charlie when I told him I had skied Stowe last winter, staying at a Youth Hostel. One of many American Youth Hostels in the 1940's recruiting New England farm houses for inexpensive overnight lodging for cyclists, skiers and hikers.

Charlie's response was unexpected. And most welcome. With his father now touring Europe, he had the temporary use of a Packard car, and all that we now needed for an exciting day in skier's paradise was snow. Without hesitating, I accepted his suggestion that we ski together. The slopes in the immediate Hanover area were not exactly challenging. And fortunately, we didn't have long to wait for snow. We both knew our remaining student days were numbered, with only a few months before receiving our Navy "Call-up" orders. Charlie to the V-12 Deck Officer's Program, and I would soon follow my brother into Navy Flight Training.

My most vivid memory of those cold winter weekends, driving the one hundred miles from Hanover to Stowe, was the unexpected shock seeing America's rural poverty close up. A grim landscape of unpainted farm houses and barns, and in towns and villages, abandoned factories and vacant retail stores. Neglected communities that had not yet overcome the ravages of the great depression.

Hanover seemed an affluent oasis in the midst of this disheartening scene, not yet revitalized by wartime prosperity. We were two privileged students familiar with living where Ghetto poverty was ubiquitous, commonplace, an expected fact of urban life in Brooklyn and the District of Columbia. What surprised us as we drove the narrow black-topped highway to Stowe was the disconnect between our bucolic vision of Vermont and what we saw. The snow covered Green Mountains were advertised as a beautiful playground for skiers, hikers and tourists. Not a dreary page out of Erskine Caldwell's *Tobacco Road*. A novel about impoverished, ignorant, Redneck Georgia.

We were not disappointed in the skiing. Greater than expected. But a greater reward of those first pre-war weekends, following hours of conversation, was discovering that Charlie and I shared a critical outsider's vision of our world.

Although we felt accepted by our classmates, with our sense of belonging on an Ivy League campus unimpaired; indeed, Charlie's intelligence, charm and infectious laughter made him extremely popular, it soon became apparent we saw everything from the outside, standing apart, looking in. Observing. Questioning. Criticizing. Taking nothing for granted.

An attribute of great value in Charlie's career.

As a Federal District Attorney, Commissioner of Public Safety and General Counsel to the District of Columbia, Dean of Howard University Law School, and a Judge on the International Court of Justice Claims Commission in the Hague, as well as partner in several prestigious Washington Law Firms, Charlie's mind cut through all specious dross, and invariably penetrated to the "root of the matter". After graduating Harvard Law School, his pro bono work in the NAACP Legal Defense Fund, mentored by Thurgood Marshall, helped win desegregation battles in Court rather than in our nation's blood-stained streets.

And so, two old friends, from ages 17 to 79, grew up together knowing great joy and tragedy. We married. Raised families. Survived wars. Witnessed riots and mass arrests. Saw inner city ghettos burning. Grieved over three assassinations, always hoping for the best. Laughing at, enjoying the "human comedy" and tragedy of a great nation unable to cope with intractable problems. We lived. Loved. Divorced. And despite many disappointments, had fun.

In 1972, following Charlie's wife's death, a soul shattering moment, Gladys Duncan, his mother, remarked I was the brother her son never had. I thought about this a moment, considering her words, and realized Charlie replaced the brother I lost in the war.

I always had a hard time keeping up with Charlie. Mentally. Or on a ski trail. Never won an argument, or a Poker game. Finally, on June 19th 2004, at Howard University Law School Chapel, before an audience of four hundred friends and associates at a memorial service conducted by the Naval Academy Chaplain, I delivered the following Eulogy having the last word in a conversation that will forever be embedded in my heart.

"It is indeed an honor to speak of sixty-two years of enduring friendship beginning in 1942 at a time when a great war united our country. Today, amidst another conflict testing our nation's pride and self-respect, I believe it is most appropriate to honor Charles Duncan by recalling what he deeply believed. Fundamental ideas essential to our survival as a democracy.

"We will never forget Charles Duncan's gentle carefree dignity, exuberant charm, laughter, devotion to friends and family, and love of that great good gift that was his long and productive life. Charles Duncan was a loving and caring man, fun to be with. Giving of himself to those in need of advice or loyalty. He did not follow the crowd and often walked alone and found himself in places few men have ever been before. His life was a passionate striving to be what no one else but Charles Duncan could be. Above all, thought-provoking. Demanding that we not merely talk to each other, but think! For God's sake think! No small achievement in today's thoughtless sound-bite culture.

"With us today to confirm this, are some of Charles Duncan's Law students. Minds touched by the flame of his thought. Or more accurately - the blow-torch cutting through all cant, specious reasoning and untenable assumptions. Charles Duncan's entire curriculum was logic, rationality and humanity. He believed with Justice Holmes's that 'The Law embodies the story of a nation's development, and in order to know what it is, we have to know what it has been, and most important, what it might become.' This he deeply and truly believed and left behind for us to think about consider, and hopefully - live by.

"Charles Duncan's favorite poet Langston Hughes once wrote: - "No man my son can batter down/ the star flung ramparts of the mind." The star flung ramparts of Charles Duncan's mind were a wonder. A surprise. A delight. And above all, an education in the majesty and nobility of the Law. Charles Duncan's passion. The Law! The Law! To be taught, practiced and defended in a nation too tolerant, Yes! - too accepting, of lawlessness.

"In 1942 we became Dartmouth classmates and after serving in the Navy, returned in 1945 as G.I. Bill students graduating in 1948. The Navy was a significant part of our education and as veterans we exchanged "Sea Stories" that evoked laughter and wonder and appreciation that we were indeed lucky to be - as the optimistic writing on Barrack walls proclaimed: - 'Home Alive in 1945'.

"Later, during years of sailing together from Chesapeake Bay to Martha's Vineyard we became 'Shipmates' acquiring that unique bonding of sailors sharing a love of going to sea.

"Twenty-five years ago sailing up the Atlantic Coast from Annapolis to Lower New York Bay, we had an all night conversation. Today, at 79, I can only retrieve part of what was said by two old friends coming of age. Having experienced war... tragedy... and challenging careers. And that night, taking turns at the helm, drinking Duncan's high-octane coffee, to my surprise, after always losing every debate and every poker game to him, we finally agreed - there are inviolable truths.

"Yes. Charles Duncan believed there are certain laws that have not been annulled or repealed. Honor to family. Loyalty to friends. Respect for the Law. Love of country. Yes indeed. How simple. How obvious. How easily forgotten... And no doubt these beliefs sustained Charles through his time of sorrow. The loss of his beloved, beautiful wife Dorothy... Then, with amazing grace, the long grief-stricken years were ended by Pamela's great love and devotion. A precious gift. A new marriage. A new life. A most precious gift.

"Charles Duncan saw the world with sighted eyes and a feeling heart. A man of compassion. Hating violence. Admiring gentleness. Kindness. Modesty. He believed in the ultimate victory of reason and morality convinced that force is always doomed to failure. And from his sense of compassion and responsibility and personal involvement emerged a great concern for alleviating suffering, injustice, discrimination.

"And finally, in closing, I am convinced Charles Duncan went raging out into the long night that is Eternity. For I can still hear his voice crying out; - protesting the dimming of the eternal ever hopeful and invincible light of our great democracy - that Charles Duncan served so well."

ELEANOR

With a high-pitched voice dissolving into a girlish giggle, shy smile, protruding teeth and awkward posture, Eleanor Roosevelt in my memory and that of all who loved her seemed beautiful, handsome and blessed with a limitless capacity to reach out and touch hearts and minds. Her devotion to our nation's under-privileged was manifest in a remarkable humane presence that inspired all who knew her as a Social Worker and President's wife. She was our nation's spokeswoman for compassion long before Spin Doctors degraded that word into a soundbite.

Eleanor was Franklin's eyes, ears and conscience conveying the emotional state of a nation surviving a deep economic depression and then enduring a devastating World War. The President's perceptions of the nation he led were focused by the realities she described with brutal honesty. Eleanor reflected what "we the people" were feeling because these feelings were also her feelings vividly described in a syndicated newspaper column "My Day". The Roosevelts were indeed our "First Family" loved and hated by a troubled nation divided between rich and poor, Left

171

and Right, Republicans and Democrats. Eleanor endured 16 years of vicious attacks against her and her husband but by their fourth term in the White House the President and his wife represented our nation's idealistic hopes for a better future.

From 1933 to 1945 I knew no other President. The Roosevelts were my other family. They inspired my generation as we went off to war. On May 28, 1942 my brother wrote from Corpus Christi Naval Air Station describing President Roosevelt's address to his graduating class. An unforgettable moment in his young and tragic life.

Before personally handing out Commissions and Wings of Gold to the new officers, the President was compelled to walk twenty feet up a small ramp leading from his parked car to the speaker's podium. The Press scrupulously observed a "gentlemen's agreement" to never show the President's infirmity and consequently few Americans had ever seen him as anything but vigorous, standing tall, or seated behind a desk charming reporters and the nation with Fireside chats.

For twenty minutes the surprised and silent graduates watched their determined President, legs locked at the knees by steel braces, his face bathed in sweat, head held high, smiling his all too familiar smile as he thrust each leg forward, advancing foot by foot, laboriously duck-walking to the Podium. Standing there almost exhausted by the effort he paused to catch his breath, grinned and raised one hand to greet the audience.

At first there were no cheers. No applause. Too moved by what they witnessed few could restrain tears and many heads turned aside to suppress sobs.

Then the President's cheery voice broke the silence and restored the festive mood. With an exaggerated gesture he wiped imaginary sweat off his forehead with the back of one hand and shook his head as if to say "I made it!"

A wave of cheers and laughter swept through the audience rising to their feet and applauding wildly. At that moment, as the applause continued for several minutes, any doubts the young Aviators had that we would win the war vanished.

Bob Schofield was one of the more flamboyant Producers I worked for as a writer and director. Bob and Louis De Rochemont created *The March of Time*, a 20 minute Newsmagazine for Theaters, a vital source of news for a nation about to enter another world war. During prohibition Bob as a Bootlegger operating from his Block Island home, acquired an astounding number of political connections solidified by generous campaign contributions. A passionate Democrat, in 1956 Bob determined that Adlai Stevenson would not be defeated again by General Eisenhower. Television would multiply the persuasive power of Stevenson's eloquent speeches. Our nation's expanding Television audience would enable the intellectual former Illinois Governor to reach more hearts and minds than in 1952 when only radio and newspapers were used. I had my doubts, but confronted by Bob's enthusiasm and the opportunity to cover a political campaign I remained silent. In 1952 I voted for Stevenson charmed by his sense of humor when he said: - referring to his business partners now managing Federal Agencies - "I only regret I have but one Law firm to give to my country."

Stevenson's speeches were masterpieces of political oratory, and when contrasted with Eisenhower's contorted syntax promised to send a man of Churchillian stature to the White House.

Stevenson and his elitist style unfortunately never connected with American voters. Stevenson lacked FDR's ability to convey large ideas in language a child could understand. His wit was applauded by educated voters but found disturbing by all who could not follow the brilliant logic of his thinking.

And on the night after his nomination, when Stevenson went to Lincoln's home to sit in Lincoln's rocking chair, few voters understood Stevenson's need to commune with the martyred President.

Schofield's idea was to cover all of Stevenson's speeches and then edit the many hours of film into thirteen and one-half minute episodes suitable for Television. "Was I interested?" he asked.

Compressing Stevenson's carefully constructed brilliant speeches to one quarter of their length while retaining their power, would be no small achievement. I hesitated. Weeks of travelling, crowded Hotels, bad food, and overnight flights were an ordeal I never enjoyed. Nevertheless, I nodded. I would be well paid.

Stevenson supporters filled the Grand Ballroom of New York's Biltmore Hotel where they dined on inedible chicken dinners in an exorbitant "Fund Raiser" demonstrating political loyalty. At one hundred dollars a plate this event was a modest precursor of the need to raise astronomical amounts of money for "sound bite" campaigns that have trivialized today's political speeches. In the pre-Kennedy era of 1956,

Roosevelt and Churchill set rhetorical standards that Stevenson often reached rousing an audience to frenzied foot-stamping cheers and applause. This is what tonight's audience paid for. The experience of being one with larger-than-life Leader who made victory seem inevitable.

As the last cups of coffee were served and the Ballroom lights dimmed, a spotlight illuminated the stage behind the speaker's Podium as the audience became silent with anticipation.

Out from behind a curtain on the side of the stage, Eleanor Roosevelt emerged approaching the Podium in her familiar hesitant walk that reminded many of a modest schoolgirl entering a classroom of strangers for the first time. The surprised and delighted audience immediately rose to their feet as a gesture of respect for her unexpected appearance and began applauding.

Eleanor seeing the audience standing and applauding stopped and turned to look back at the curtain behind her and began applauding what she thought was the arrival of what she assumed was someone very important. Perhaps the Guest of Honor.

After what seemed like several minutes peering into the wings offstage and applauding the appearance of someone who did not step out from behind the curtain, Eleanor turned and stared out at the audience who began to laugh and cheer and shout and make quite evident that the applause was for her. Eleanor Roosevelt. Our nations most beloved First Lady.

Embarrassed when she realized this affectionate greeting was for her, and her alone, Eleanor shook her head as if to say "No! No! You're mistaken!"

Then she sat in a chair behind the Speaker's Podium, her hands resting in her lap, and blushed like a shy schoolgirl unaccustomed to being the center of attention.

Fifty three years later I do not remember a word of Adlai Stevenson's brilliant audience-rousing speech. I vaguely remember the audience's enthusiastic response to his incisive rhetoric that is almost unknown today.

What I will never forget is the schoolgirl blush on the cheeks of a truly great and beloved woman who was so much a part of my childhood.

HIS NAME WAS MUDD

Entering the Grand Ballroom of the Hollywood Roosevelt Hotel one Fall evening in 1949 to attend a Screenwriters Guild meeting I was not surprised by the charged atmosphere. The usual jokes and laughter were replaced by a strange and unexpected silence. This exuberant group of talented and hardworking writers seemed unusually subdued waiting for the meeting to begin. As I glanced around at my fellow Guild members, it seemed a contagion of dread filled the room. The Screenwriters, some quite well-known, seemed like little boys again, lost in the dark.

Tonight we assembled to discuss a document placed on the meeting's Agenda by handsome, grey-haired Dudley Nichols, Hollywood's most distinguished and courageous writer, role model and Mentor. A document a majority of members did not want the Guild to consider or endorse. And that was to sign and submit an "Amicus Curiae" Friend of the Court Brief to the United States Supreme Court requesting that they review and hopefully reverse the Contempt Citations of ten Screenwriters refusing to answer questions of the notorious House Un-

American Activities Committee. Without a review and reversal of the Indictments the Blacklisted writers would be jailed for as much as twelve months. 1949 was a bad year for Hollywood and all who worked in the film industry. The Playwright Lillian Hellman called it a "Scoundrel Time". An era ravaged by a Blacklist that destroyed careers and lifetime friendships. Many actors, writers and directors named names to the House Un-American Activities Committee to maintain or regain their employability. The wartime years of Soviet-American Friendship had given way to Cold War paranoia and publicity-seeking Congressmen found Communist propaganda in such delightful films as Disney's *Snow White and the Seven Dwarfs*.

Cooperative committee witnesses informing to demonstrate loyalty to our government while protecting their careers paid an enormous price in personal pride and self-respect. Clifford Odets, Budd Schulberg, Elia Kazan were but a few of many truly gifted talents who then endured a lifetime of scorn for naming names.

Those named and cited by the committee were often guilty of nothing more than attending a Progressive political Rally. Donating to a subversive group listed by Congress could result in personal, financial or marital disaster. Being named by some old friend or former associate caused several suicides.

"Scoundrel Time" was a time of Loyalty Oaths as a condition of employment by governments, universities and defense industries. Telephones were tapped without Court Orders, Postmasters were required to intercept foreign mail addressed to suspected Communist sympathizers like Playwright

Arthur Miller, and only the Association of American Librarians displayed moral courage by refusing to list for the FBI Left-Wing books being checked-out by disloyal Pinkos or Fellow Travelers.

In the Fall of 1949 no one anticipated that the anti-Communist Witch Hunt madness soon to be intensified and exploited by Senator Joe McCarthy would ever burn-out and ultimately destroy the political careers of the Witch Hunters. In Hollywood in 1949, donating money, attending a political meeting, or signing a Petition could destroy a career. "Keep your head down, mouth shut, and your bowels open" was the sardonic wisdom of the day for all hoping to retain their jobs in the film industry.

Dudley Nichols and others recruiting signatures for the Amicus Curiae Brief prefaced their remarks by saying that although they shared few of the political beliefs of the ten cited writers they did without reservation support the principals for which they were willing to go to jail. Freedom of speech, thought, and conscience protected by the Constitution of the United States was under siege. To remain silent, to refuse to sign the Brief asking the Court to review and reverse the ten contempt Citations would make us accomplices of those attempting to destroy our freedom.

I recall several other eloquent speeches followed by scattered applause. And then, only the silence of a Funeral Home. No one rose to reply to the impassioned speakers. There was nothing more to be said. Without further discussion, the meeting adjourned as most of the members hurried out of the room. Perhaps embarrassed. But certainly in their minds, cautious, prudent, men with families to support. The Amicus

Curiae Brief lay on a table in front of the room and proceeding to it was a line of other writers of all political persuasions waiting their turn to sign the Brief. Their names and exact number survive only in the Supreme Court's Archives and I am proud to say my name is among them.

The ironic Law of Unexpected Consequences seemed to protect the careers of those who despite the apparent risk signed the Brief. "Friends of the Court" often found this identity an asset giving them preference over other writers in Hollywood's competitive job market.

Which confirms Winston Churchill's statement that in the long run "Doing right is always the right thing to do."

The Justices of the Supreme Court, sensitive to Cold War hysteria, declined to hear the Appeals of the demonized Hollywood Ten sentenced to between ten and twelve months in Federal prisons for refusing to answer a Congressional Committee's questions.

As model prisoners the writers were respected by other prisoners for not being snitches. In the prison culture, unlike society outside its walls, no one is more despised than an Informer. The writers served their sentences working in the prison Infirmary, Library, and classrooms during that enlightened era when rehabilitation of convicts was still considered as important a goal as punishment.

Ring Lardner Jr., Screenwriter of *MASH* explained his refusal to violate his deepest beliefs, his conscience, going to prison rather than answer Committee Chairman Parnell Thomas's questions. "Yes. I can answer your questions, sir. But if I do I will hate myself in the morning."

Six months later, Parnell Thomas, convicted of padding his Congressional payroll was assigned to cleaning out the chicken coops at the Federal prison in Danbury, Connecticut where the writers now serving time there could only ponder poetic justice when separating their personal tragedies from utter, unbelievable farce.

Their fate, and the personal tragedies of the thousands of other Blacklisted performers, writers and directors were not fictional scenes in a screenplay or television drama. Their loss of homes, families, and indeed lives really happened to honorable men and women holding on to their most precious possession, their integrity, no matter the cost.

In Arthur Miller's play *The Crucible*, John Proctor, refusing to name names by crying Witch against his neighbors, chose to die rather than live and besmirch his good name. "Because I can not have another in my life!" he cried out. "How may I live without my name? I have given you my soul: leave me my name!"

Many Blacklisted writers like Dalton Trumbo and Ring Lardner Jr., survived by adopting other names working at reduced fees for producers exploiting their predicament. Some directors with international reputations like Joseph Losey, Carl Foreman and Jules Dassin fled to England, Italy and Greece producing films that were financial and artistic triumphs.

But for actors like Lloyd Bridges there was no alternative to waiting for phone calls that never came. Inexplicably, after what many considered a breakthrough role in *High Noon*, Bridges was suddenly unemployable. Bridges had participated in Hollywood's "bleeding-heart" culture signing Petitions, contributing to fund-raisers, and attending political Rallys. A life-style shared with others who were Liberal, Progressive or simply idealistic as Sunday School teachers practicing the Golden Rule. When Blacklisted it was impossible to determine which Petition, fund-raiser, or political Rally added your name to the list of Fellow-Travelers cited by the House Un-American Activities Committee.

For those who never donated a dollar or attended a political meeting, associating with friends who did was sufficient to destroy a career through guilt by association, a concept previously used to justify hanging 19 Witches in Salem Massachusetts in 1692.

After ten destructive years the Congressional committee and their Hollywood supporters retreated enabling courageous producers like Otto Preminger and Ivan Tors to ignore the Blacklist. Lloyd Bridges who had been working as a Liquor salesman was now cast by Tors as the lead in his successful *Sea Hunt* television series.

For serious actors performing gave dignity and meaning to their lives. To act and be potent on stage, or before the camera, was to be fully alive. Denied an opportunity to act was to lose the center of one's being - what and who you are. The worst death of all.

And your name determined your employability enabling you to live the life you loved, one worth all the sweat and blood enduring the pain filled years of an acting career.

Your name was your most precious possession.

Producer Larry Jacobson financed the adventure series *Water World* on the strength of Lloyd Bridges' newly acquired "bankable name". His popular *Sea*

Hunt TV series was in its fourth Syndicated re-run making Bridges a recognized Star. Handsome, and versatile, Bridges attracted audiences advertisers wanted to reach.

For two years I wrote 26 *Water World* scripts relating a variety of sea-adventures that had everything an armchair seafarer could hope for. Bridges' enthusiasm and energy delivered the right blend of information and entertainment receiving high ratings and numerous re-runs over the next five years.

One of our most dramatic programs, *His Name is Mudd* told the story of Dr. Samuel Mudd an innocent Physician who was convicted as one of the Lincoln conspirators for setting the broken leg of John Wilkes Booth, Lincoln's assassin. Sentenced to life imprisonment, Dr. Mudd was banished to Fort Jefferson, 68 miles west of Key West, at the far end of a string of Coral Keys, an outpost on one of the Dry Tortugas guarding the Gulf of Mexico.

Circled by a 70 foot wide Shark-infested Moat, the eight foot thick walls of the "Gibralter of the Gulf" rise fifty feet around a half mile perimeter inspiring the thought: "Those who enter here leave all hope behind."

Wrongfully convicted in the hysteria following Lincoln's death, Dr. Mudd was a prisoner at the Fort from 1865 to 1869. Pardoned by President Andrew Johnson for his courageous work saving lives during a Yellow Fever epidemic, Dr. Mudd spent most of his prison time in irons chained to the wall of a damp cell and was only released to work as a doctor when the Post Surgeon, Major Joseph Smith died.

For acting as a Physician, setting Booth's broken leg, Doctor Mudd, denied the right to testify in his own defense, and despite 60 witnesses testifying on his behalf, was found guilty of conspiracy by a Military Commission.

When arrested, Dr. Mudd, on orders from Secretary of War Stanton, wore a canvas bag over his head tied around the neck with a hole for breathing. Brought into Court in chains, unshaven and disheveled, Dr. Mudd looked guilty long before he was convicted. To prevent Dr. Mudd from applying for a Civilian trial he was transported to a Military prison. America's "Devil's Island". Fort Jefferson.

"His Name is Mudd" became a description of anyone demonized by inflamed public opinion. After Lincoln's assassination over-zealous Witch Hunters committed Judicial Murder ignoring a Judge's Writ of Habeas Corpus and hanging Mary E. Suratt who was only guilty of renting a room to John Wilkes Booth. One Conspirator was convicted for holding Booth's horse outside Ford theater.

Deprived of a good name, everyone is vulnerable to Lynch mob hysteria and madness. From Salem Massachusetts in 1692 to Hollywood's Blacklists in 1949, unprincipled accusers have destroyed reputations with impunity. Presumption of innocence until proven guilty by a Jury of peers has become a legal anachronism.

The cold damp cell where Dr. Mudd was chained from 1865 to 1869 was crowded with cameras, lights, and sound recorders and a production crew eager to film the closing scene of our program and return to Key West's modern comforts. The heat of our lights in the confined space added to our discomfort and keeping Lloyd Bridges' face free of perspiration when in front of the camera was no easy task.

Movie crews concentrating on their separate yet coordinated jobs rarely pay attention to what performers say. Their concern is with proper lighting, clean, audible sound, and smooth camera movements rewarded with good usable "takes". An efficient crew moves on effortlessly from each complicated camera "set-up" with a minimum of delay warming the cost-conscious heart of their producer. Yet today, on that forbidding island far out in the Gulf of Mexico, spooked by the cruelty and terror enclosed inside the walls of this old fortress prison, everyone in that now over-heated cell listened intently as Bridges delivered his lines. He told of 370 prisoners dying of Yellow Fever on this remote island and of the survivors saved by Dr. Mudd petitioning President Andrew Johnson in 1869 to unconditionally grant him a Pardon. He told of another, this time unsuccessful Petition submitted to President Nixon in 1968 by Dr. Richard Mudd hoping to restore his Grandfather's good name. He asked that the President declare Dr. Mudd innocent, or grant him a new trial in a Civil court.

For a man can have only one name in his life. And that name must be free of all stigma.

Asking "What's in a name?" Bridges quoted Othello's immortal lines:

"Good name in man and woman, dear Lord, is the immediate jewel of their souls: Who steals my purse steals trash; 'tis something, nothing; But he who filches from me my good name Robs me of that which not enriches him, And makes me poor indeed."

Our response in that small hot prison cell was an extended moment of stunned silence. A choked sob. And tears. And remembered fears. Exhausted by the surge of now suddenly released feelings recalled from his Blacklisted past, Lloyd Bridges stepped out from behind the blinding lights to await our reaction. Then, suddenly, the powerful emotions evoked in all of us by his performance exploded into wild applause. Loud cheers.

Art and Life, at this one instant of creative magic came together to arouse in each heart the dark terror of being unjustly accused. Humiliated. Disgraced by the loss of a good name.

MAX

Madame Boulanger's love of her native language was only exceeded by her passion for everything French. As her student at Madison High I became an avid Francophile. Dumas, de Maupassant, Victor Hugo and Balzac captured my imagination. "La Belle France" became my fountainhead of Western civilization and could do no wrong. Twenty years later, anticipating filming in France, I practiced my conversational skills at the Alliance Francaise where Camus, Malraux and Sartre were cultural icons as important as the actresses Jeanne Moreau and Brigette Bardot with or without her Bikini.

My admiration for France peaked when in Flight Training with French Naval Cadets I joined them singing *la Marseilles* after reading General Charles de Gaulle's speech delivered at Notre Dame Cathedral the day of Paris' liberation: "Paris has been liberated by her own people..." the Free French Leader said. "With the help and support of the whole of France, that is to say of fighting France... the true France, the Eternal France."

A special kind of jubilation was evoked by that patriotic song and De Gaulle's words when I recalled the June 1940 photograph showing a victorious German Army parading down the Champs Elysee past the Arc de Triumph as crowds of sobbing French men and women watched. Then in 1945, after five years of bloodshed the good guys won. The bad guys lost. God was in his heaven and all was well with the world that again included the glory-filled nation that General De Gaulle described as "Fighting France... the True France... Eternal France."

For ten years I shared De Gaulle's heroic vision of a triumphant France resisting German occupiers until my friend Max Rainat suggested I read what Jean Paul Sartre wrote immediately after the Liberation of France by English, Canadian and American Armies. "A past which fills New York and London with pride was for Paris marked with shame and despair."

Sartre versus De Gaulle. Two versions of History.

History is written by the Victors, hi-jacked some say to create a usable past satisfying a sense of national dignity and honor. But according to my friend Max, France played only a minor role in Germany's defeat and after the war created a myth about the contribution of the Resistance and the Free French forces led by General De Gaulle.

The true story of wartime France, he insisted, tells of a French government collaborating with their conquerors becoming co-administrators of Hitler's Final Solution. Most French citizens survived by moral compromises. Few were Résistants. A noble few redeemed the honor of France by never collaborating, risking their lives to resist the evil acts of a Government subservient to Nazi rule exploiting defeat to impose a Fascist New Order on France.

Max was one of the noble few. He survived. And he had a story to tell no French Publisher would even read.

I was introduced to Max in 1951 by Jean Oser, a Director at Warner Brothers who hired me to write about the transformation of the impoverished Marbial Valley in Haiti. Jean fled Nazi persecution in Berlin with his actress wife Ellen, resuming their film careers in Paris until June 1940 when as an undocumented foreigner he joined the French Foreign Legion to escape internment, serving as a soldier in North Africa. Ellen survived the war in Paris by not wearing an identifying Yellow Star, sheltered by Righteous Gentiles who risked death helping her evade Gendarmes enforcing French Racial Laws.

In November 1942 the Americans invaded North Africa. Jean Oser demobilized from the Legion enlisted in the US Army and soon was directing and editing Training Films at the Signal Corps Studio in Astoria Long Island. Irwin Shaw a writer at Astoria remembered Oser as a flamboyant European who rejected the discomforts of an Army Barracks to live in a Manhattan Hotel reporting for duty every morning in a Taxi. Oser had style. Was charming. And denied himself few of the luxuries available to a Refugee who had mastered the art of survival.

Max Rainat arrived in New York, a nephew of Oser's friend Boris Vermont who passed his responsibility for Max on to Jean who then asked me, since I spoke French, to "look after the boy." Help him get settled.

Oser, like a Circus Ringmaster was adept at directing at a breathless pace, juggling past, present and future, crowding three lives into one lifetime. I found it impossible to say "No."

Max Rainat who did not use his full name for many years, was no boy. And never a hapless refugee. What he was, was an intelligent highly creative Force of Nature.

And so began a friendship that endured forty years.

Thanks to the Real Estate pages of the New York Times I found Max an apartment on Irving Place adjacent to Pete's Tavern once frequented by the writer O'Henry. Over a Beer beneath O'Henry's portrait, Max explained he had worked as a Journalist, published a book of poems, written screenplays, and now needed a job. Uncle Boris had no interest in supporting him.

35 West 45th street housed the United States Information Agency's "Voice of America" broadcast studios where I arranged a job interview for Max. To my astonishment he was hired by the French Language Desk to broadcast about Life in the United States. A startling achievement at a time of endless FBI background checks for government employees. A hiring that Max accepted without surprise. He was a qualified Journalist.

Max had an apartment and a job and I had more than met the responsibility evaded by his Uncle Boris. And now that long summer of 1954 I was off to direct a film in Greenland and for many months heard not a word from my friend. Until one Fall evening, strolling Fifth Avenue past Lord and Taylor's Department store across the street from the New York Public Library, I stopped to watch a Window Designer supervise the dressing of windows for next week's Thanksgiving display. New York Department Stores celebrate holidays with great creativity and as I watched the window dressers at work I realized the Supervisor was Max.

Yes, he said, he was still broadcasting for the Voice of America and got this night-time job walking into the Manager's office with a sketch pad of ideas for windows. A flamboyant Parisian speaking accented English, Max could charm birds out of trees when he smiled. And so for the next few years Max designed Holiday windows for several Fifth Avenue department stores.

Then writing a series of animated films for Caravel Studios I needed a Storyboard artist to visualize my scripts. Jack Semple, Caravel's Chief Animator glanced at Max's sketchbook and hired him without a quibble over salary. Boris' nephew now had three jobs with more to come.

In 1955 when directing *Gentlemen Start Your Engines* at Indianapolis, Max asked to work as my Unit Manager responsible for the logistics of budget and schedule and crew. With remarkable ease everything we needed was where it was needed when it was needed. But for Max wet-nursing a movie crew was no challenge and he refused to go on location again.

For the next two years Max worked as a Political cartoonist for the Detroit Free Press mailing me examples of his sardonic wit until one day he arrived at my home driving a Ford Thunderbird accompanied by his wife Joyce.

Detroit was not Paris. He had enough of mid-western respectability and to my astonishment had purchased the "Esther Perry", a forty-five foot sailboat and was off to the Bahamas and his next career as a Charter Boat Captain. Joyce would mix drinks, do the cooking and he already had several reservations for cruising next winter.

"Do you know how to sail?" I asked.

"No," he said. "But you'll show me what I need to know."

And so I did.

A series of post cards soon informed me the "Esther Perry" had successfully motored down the Inter-Coastal Waterway to Coral Gables, Florida, and for a year I heard nothing from Max until a book arrived in the mail. *Les Isles de Juin*, a Best Seller, published in France describing Max's adventures cruising the Bahamas and the Coastal Waterway satisfying an armchair sailor's vicarious need of exotic travel.

The book also contained several surprises.

It was dedicated: "To Norman Weissman, the writer, the sailor, and the friend."

And for the first time I learned his complete name. Max Rainat Desleves.

France's post-war years were years of silence for veterans, refugees and displaced persons who rarely talked about the horrors they experienced, and it was considered tactful not to ask. Grievous wounds were private and never discussed. Reading the Publisher's Blurb on the book jacket I learned that in 1945 Max had been the youngest non-commissioned officer in the French Air Force, a well-known journalist and filmmaker, and also star of the popular *Ici New York* broadcasts. Speaking three languages and three regional dialects Max was also described as an accomplished sports car racer and pilot.

When France's gift to the New World decided to become a U.S. citizen I accompanied Max to the swearing-in ceremony. And then in keeping with all previous surprises Max announced his return to Paris to work for RDTFC, Radio Diffusion Télévision Francais, the government broadcasting Service. His old Boss, Andre Malraux, now Minister of Culture, was hiring former Résistants as a reward for wartime patriotism. Max, a decorated "Compagnon de La Libération " was a war hero.

Respecting Max's disciplined privacy I sensed that locked up in his memory was a past he refused to recall. One of the few personal details he shared concerned a Grandmother raising him in Saint Cyr, a town housing a Military Academy where his Russian Grandfather, a Jewish Officer, trained during the first World War.

Max's few lapses in strict secrecy yielded several admissions.

Yes. He came to New York using an abbreviated name for his own protection. And yes, in 1940, at fifteen he had been an early Résistant and after four years risking his life to make La Libération possible, served in the French Air Force.

Max, like many of his generation attempted to escape his memory of Vichy France's disgraceful history. He rejected the heroic myth that became the false narrative of France's shameful years .

He knew better. He was there. And he wrote a book about what he knew.

Before returning to Paris in 1965, Max gave me his unpublished manuscript *Les Imposteurs*, a book French Publishers rejected. Denial of the truth about France's war-time behavior persisted until 1995 when President Jacques Chirac accepted national responsibility for the French government saying "These black hours will stain our history forever and are an injury to our past and our traditions. Yes, this criminal madness was supported by the French and the French state."

Les Imposteurs, narrated by a Résistant like Max tells of the cruelty of France's Militia. The Milice combined the horrors of the Gestapo with Mafia brutality zealously persecuting Jews, torturing and murdering opponents of France's New Order. They plundered the assets of anyone described by Racial Laws as foreign and subject to deportation to German Concentration Camps. 90,000 Jews, including 4000 children, were transported from France in 84 railroad Convoys assembled by the French police. 30,000 Résistants were executed and 20,000 disappeared opposing this national dishonor. French men, women and children died sheltering victims of France's moral bankruptcy.

In 1940, as La Résistance began, adolescent boys and girls after demonstrating reliability as Couriers or messengers, escorted escaped POW's, evading capture along a network of rural farm houses and villages leading to freedom in Spain or Switzerland. As British and American Air Forces intensified attacks against European targets, one day losing more than eight hundred Airmen, it rained Aviators, and of those parachuting into France, fifty per cent returned to England to fly and fight again.

More than 6000 Résistants were executed for
guiding 5000 Evaders over the Pyrenees Mountains
or across the English Channel to freedom.

It was a heart-stopping game for teen-age boys
or girls to escort tall, well-fed American or English
"Evaders" in ill-fitting civilian clothes, showing
forged documents at checkpoints where patriotic
Gendarmes, but never the Milice, sometimes ignored
the deception.

Travelling by bicycle or train, posing as fathers
and sons, or girl friends, Evaders and their French-
speaking young Guides were often betrayed
by citizens supporting Germany's New Order.
Frenchmen denouncing neighbors and confiscating
Jewish property reversed France's historic tradition of
giving sanctuary to all fleeing persecution or capture.
For Max Rainat and other Résistants, the nation he
loved and was willing to die for had been corrupted
beyond recognition. Informers and Collaborators
outnumbered Patriots.

Anticipating the 1944 Invasion, Les Résistants
attacked railroads and bridges limiting the German
Army's ability to transport and supply troops defending
the Normandy beaches. And with La Libération
and Freedom spreading across France, there also
began the indiscriminate killing of Collaborators
and Informers. For teen-age Résistants, executing
Collaborators, shaving the heads of naked girls for
sleeping with German soldiers, the Vigilante purge of
more than ten thousand Traitors became an indelible
lifetime memory.

After reading *Les Imposteurs* I understood France's
passion for myth and silence. A need marked by

memories evoking in tormented souls, a continuing dialogue with pain, horror and shame.

Yes. As *Les Imposteurs* relates - the only thing worse than dying for your Country - is killing for your Country.

In 1967 I received another of Max's startling surprises. The announcement of his marriage to the Baroness Clarmont-Pichon, in Paris, on the 5th of September. Soon an impassioned letter arrived describing his bride with what appeared to be the ravings of a Poet in love. However Max did not exaggerate. Mariel was charming, beautiful, a talented singer and a designer and fabricator of magnificent Wall Tapestries as well as a passionate gardener.

I was scheduled to direct a film at the Pasteur Institute in May and asked Max to assemble a crew and work with me as Unit Manager. We met at the Airport and drove to his apartment at 44 Rue Saint-louis-en-L'Isle with what I thought was restrained excitement.

Max delighted in confronting friends with the unexpected. Divorce. Re-marriage. And now a proud Papa introducing his step children, a boy and a girl, handsome University students. Max's war-time Résistant pride surfaced as he explained Marigrene and her brother were now demonstrating against government restrictions on student financial aid and other failed social policies.

Student riots in China, Japan, Mexico and the United States filled the world's TV screens in May 1968. A violent Cultural War between generations produced scenes of burning automobiles and masked Police wielding clubs amidst clouds of Tear gas. Flaming gasoline bombs shattered store windows as harassed Firemen fought fires. Sirens and flashing Ambulance lights evoked images of Civil War as the injured were transported to Hospital under the watchful eye of TV cameras. Max was delighted. Students were "shaking things up". Challenging the Old Farts. The established Elite who were only good at seizing and maintaining political power. Incredibly, after hundreds of students were arrested, a significant part of France joined the strike. Parents, professors and labor unions now accompanied twenty thousand demonstrating students. Farmers sent food. Car pools replaced buses and the Metro. And De Gaulle went to Baden-Baden Germany to ask NATO to help quell the demonstration.

But soon, without garbage pick-ups and public transportation, fear of Civil War increased public support for De Gaulle's harsh Law and Order response. When students, some of Jewish parentage were expelled from Universities, thousands of Parisians marched and sang:

"Nous sommes tous des Juifs Allemands -- We are all German Jews."

A few days later Max appeared at work distraught. Marigrene had disappeared. Last night's student demonstrations had been violent with gunfire and Tear gas and rumors of dead students thrown in the Seine like the Algerians several years ago. And even more disturbing a complete blackout had been ordered on TV reporting.

The official response was nothing happened. The blood-stained riots were a non-event out of George Orwell's foreboding novel 1984.

For two days we searched every Hospital in Paris for his step-daughter. On the final night of our quest, with Max resigned to Marigrene's death, we found her recovering from an asthma attack and pneumonia induced by military-strength CN gas. In an adjacent bed, her boyfriend, his back cut open by metal fragments of exploding gas grenades as he fled the Police, almost bled to death before receiving the transfusions that saved his life.

Rioting Police escalated student opposition into a civic disturbance for Officials more concerned with maintaining Law and Order than listening to dissenters. The 1968 demonstrations replayed the tragedy of Frenchmen killing Frenchmen during La Libération . They repeated what often occurred during the many Civil Wars that divided France into those in power and the powerless who were killed with impunity.

General De Gaulle, who refused to accept the Armistice in June 1940, leading Free French Résistants to La Libération in August 1944, was Max's mentor and representative of all that was truly great about France. Now this courageous champion of French civilization behaved like a frightened politician using unrestrained violence to hold office.

Max was devastated. His hero had fallen. Insisting "this is not what we liberated France for" he resigned from RDTFC rather than broadcast the official story line that the Police only did what was necessary to restore calm.

One of our last European encounters occurred when working in Munich in 1979. Max drove from Paris motivated as much by the anticipated delights of the Fasching holiday, as by our friendship. Costumed and masked revelers drinking and singing and dancing in the streets created a surprising Mardi Gras reversal of Germanic propriety. Max, a man of modest height, dragged off to dance to the point of exhaustion by tall blonde Valkyries of unlimited energy, was no longer the serious French intellectual burdened by the world's tragedies. He was a happy boy again, having fun. His pain-filled past forgotten at that moment. Or so I thought.

Max, his face glistening with sweat, insisted we find the infamous Brown House and drink at the Beer Hall where Hitler began his political career. It would be a visit Max often imagined. At fifteen he was beaten by the Gestapo and, after a few days released with bruises and a warning to behave. On his first trip to Germany he wanted to see where the Nazi terror began.

The Brown House was no different from numerous other Munich Beer Halls. Parallel rows of wooden tables were scarred by pounding Beer Steins as intoxicated patrons combined continuous drinking with song. An endless parade of buxom waitresses grasping as many as three Steins in each hand, hurried from table to table to serve what appeared to be insatiable thirst. After consuming several Steins of heavy dark Beer Max said he would sing me a song taught him by an English pilot. One of many Evaders who successfully fled France.

Seated at the end of our table we had been ignored by signing revelers accompanying music played by a four-piece Band. Max rose to his feet wearing a Blue Regimental Blazer displaying a small "Cross of Lorraine" on his breast pocket, a military decoration in his lapel. At that moment, he was France. He raised his Stein as if toasting an unseen presence, and began singing. Softly at first. And then louder. Much louder. Soon attracting an audience.

"Hitler, had no balls at all / Goering had two - but they were small / Himmler - had something similar / But Hitler - had no balls at all!"

A long moment of silence. Then raucous laughter, followed by requests that Max repeat the song. Teach the audience the English words so everyone at our table could sing with him. I was relieved. This new generation of Germans were definitely different. And Max, at that moment, had scored another victory in a war that in his unquiet memory would never end.

A thick folder in my file cabinet is filled with our letters. Always a diligent correspondent the months and years between our encounters were enriched with personal views on the ever-changing events in Europe. Max's hilarious political cartoons depicting Marshall Plan French Brothels giving S & H Green Trading Stamps to Patrons also included jokes about frugal General De Gaulle ordering a three day rental instead of buying an expensive and magnificent State coffin.

In 1981, after a worrisome interval without a letter, a cartoon arrived with news that Max chose not to express in words but rather with a final laugh at Fate. With sardonic joy a courageous Résistant gave notice of his departure, taking leave of a world he loved and served so well.

MEL

At Key West's Pier House Chart Room, around the corner from Hemingway's "Sloppy Joe's" Bar where work is the curse of the drinking classes, a crew of hard-working young adventurers met every evening to sustain their dream of finding a fortune in Spanish Gold scattered on nearby reefs.

Drop-outs from conventional careers, they held on to their abiding faith that the underwater Mother Lode of gold they sought really existed, and no doubt, tomorrow was the day they would find it. Like the California '49ers and the frost-bitten Gold Miners of the Klondike, these obsessed fortune hunters initiated a new Gold Rush beneath the seas off Key West. Though tourism and Cruise ship visits displaced Piracy, smuggling and shipwrecking as the seaport's main activity, these impoverished Scuba Divers and Salvors living on Food Stamps and hope fit right in with Key West's laid-back anything-goes lifestyle. Hard-drinking, raucous, they were outcasts who after many disappointments scouring the surrounding waters were derided as foolish dreamers who refused to accept defeat.

Five deaths and sixteen years later, triumphing over greedy Bureaucracies, the disdain of Archaeologists who called them outlaws, a hostile press, virulent character assassination, unscrupulous Claim Jumpers and turbulent seas, they retrieved from the wreck of the Spanish galleon Nuestra Señora de Atocha more than four hundred Million dollars in gold, silver and emeralds.

A quintessential American story. Self-reliant independent individuals overcoming outrageous obstacles through perseverance, character and the ability to make dreams come true. Experiencing the heights and depths of heart-breaking failure and intoxicating success, this happy-go-lucky crew of Salvors were never earthbound. Transformed by triumph and tragedy, they became uncommon men and women with remarkable stories to tell.

In August 1971, at Key West to film another episode in Lloyd Bridges' *Water World* TV series, I returned to my room at the Pier House Motel to recover from an exhausting day. My sleep was interrupted by a phone call from Lloyd insisting I come down to the bar to meet someone special. Someone he admired. A man obsessed with a fantastic dream. Mel Fisher. A tall, larger than life presence presiding over a crowded table of loyal followers. A rag-tag crew of dream-sharers. "True Believers" willing to endure privation, low or non-existent pay, and years of heart-breaking disappointment diving on wrecks from rust-bucket salvage ships, risking death with obsolete SCUBA gear.

Fisher, a former Chicken farmer who founded California's first Dive Shop in 1950, introduced Scuba Diving as a new exotic sport. Selling his farm, he then supported his family guiding divers he equipped and trained in the waters around California's Channel Islands.

Lloyd's highly rated *Sea Hunt* TV series, along with Mel Fisher's photographic coverage of his diving excursions, aired on local TV, popularized the adventures made possible by the invention of SCUBA gear. In 1963, moving his activities to Sebastian Inlet, Florida, Fisher's retrieval of 1000 gold doubloons from the wreck of a 1715 Spanish Treasure Fleet made him a celebrity inspiring a National Geographic article titled: "Drowned Galleons Yield Spanish Gold."

That memorable summer evening in 1971, Lloyd and Mel traded "sea-stories" exuberantly relating their astonishing underwater adventures to an appreciative audience. Fisher was a gifted story-teller. Soft-spoken. Matter-of-fact. With a talent for making incredible experiences believable. As I was now also writing and editing Brooks Fleig's feature length *SCUBA* to be narrated by Lloyd, I was unhappy not recording Fisher's perhaps exaggerated tales. True or false they provided exciting material for future films. I also regretted that budget limitations prevented Mel's ongoing quest for treasure from becoming another episode in the *Water World* TV series we were now filming.

For the next sixteen years I followed Mel Fisher's exploits reported in National Geographic articles and documentaries. From his arrival in Key West in 1970, to the retrieval of the Atocha's Mother Lode of gold in 1985, Fisher's persistent struggle and ultimate success demonstrated incredible human resilience. He seemed a heroic character in a Greek or Shakespearean tragedy. Five SCUBA divers, including his son, died in pursuit of his quest. A dream many critics thought impossible. At times unable to support his family he was derided. Insulted. Humiliated.

"Would you buy a used shipwreck from this chicken farmer?" taunted him, his wife and children. Scandal-mongering journalists inventing controversial headlines called him a scam artist, a liar, and a crook cheating investors by seeding off-shore reefs with worthless artifacts.

Shakespeare's "slings and arrows of outrageous fortune" best describes what Mel Fisher endured. He survived without anger or bitterness prolonged IRS and SEC investigations, the dishonoring of salvage leasing agreements by Federal and State governments, the animosity of archeologists who accused him of plundering historic sites, and finally, after sixteen heart-breaking years, diluting his great moment of triumph, the unbearable sorrow of personal tragedy.

Fisher's corporation, Treasure Salvors, Inc. never exhausted an ongoing need for more investors. Between 1970 and 1985, Fisher raised and spent more than 7.1 million dollars scouring Key West's off-shore reefs. Offering thousand dollar shares, Mel's flamboyant charm evoking Gold Fever continued to attract new investors. Participating in a real adventure, finding hidden treasure promoted by Mel's verbal leaps into the unknown, proved irresistible. Sharing Mel's dream, win or lose, seemed sufficient reward to anyone willing to risk failure.

During the disappointing years when the Atocha's Mother Lode was not found, and months when Mel's divers were shore bound without money for food or fuel, Mel continued his desperate search for financing. Displaying artifacts recovered in 1963, Mel never stopped selling shares in his great dream. And an enthralled public, responding to Fisher's passionate belief in his enterprise, continued to invest.

Mel's talent for evoking the imaginations of potential investors, bringing them into a dream world to share his vision of enormous wealth, made him vulnerable to critics who resented a Californian's intrusion on their Turf. His true but often exaggerated tales seemed to confirm a belief he was nothing more than a Con Man. A disciple of P.T. Barnum who proclaimed "There's a sucker born every minute."

Mel loved wheeling and dealing. A talented entrepreneur, promoting new enterprises, persuading investors that the exotic dreams flowing from his keen intelligence and active imagination were real seemed a passion as great as his quest for the Atocha. Many called him a "Pied Piper" leading followers to financial ruin. So intense were these savage efforts at personal destruction that several otherwise rational citizens pledged not to cease trashing his reputation until they put Mel Fisher in jail.

There was blood on the water inciting a feeding frenzy of scandal-mongering led by Forbes Magazine, the Wall Street Journal and the Miami Herald. "The only sharks we encountered were on land," Mel joked, as the SEC began a long, expensive and futile investigation of Treasure Salvors, inc. At a final Hearing Mel amicably signed a consent decree pledging not to sell unregistered securities. A settlement affirming his innocence.

Using an unresolved Tax dispute as justification, the IRS later impounded Treasure Salvors financial records compelling an already strapped Mel to somehow raise more money to raise liens on all his property.

And then there were real Pirates to defeat. Bureaucratic Pirates who never got their feet wet and were finally vanquished in Court; and armed sea-going pirates, Claim Jumpers who were jailed for firing on his crews, threatening to break legs, kidnapping two of Mel's supervisors while stealing recovered treasure.

In the 1960's, before moving to Key West, Fisher salvaged shipwrecks off Sebastian Inlet well inside Florida's three mile sovereignty limit. Under a 1963 lease granting him exclusive rights to this search area, Mel shared 25 per cent of all recovered treasure with the state. After moving to Key West in 1970 to search for the Atocha wreck thirty miles off-shore, Florida immediately extended State sovereignty to include Mel's new area demanding a share of all recovered treasure.

After a protracted and expensive Court battle, Fisher defeated Florida's expanded sovereignty claim only to be confronted by the Federal government's insistence on jurisdiction. Resorting to the ancient Law of Admiralty, Fisher claimed salvage rights with the Court finding that "Treasure Salvors successfully saved property of considerable, historic, archeological and monetary value... and the Court therefore holds that the plaintiff, Treasure Salvors, inc. shall be awarded all the articles it has recovered since the inception of this lawsuit as compensation for its expenses and an award for superlative salvage services."

After years of unremitting legal struggle, justice prevailed. Reluctantly, confronted by Federal Marshals armed with guns and a Court Order, the state of Florida returned all previously confiscated treasure. A long-delayed moment of personal vindication for Mel Fisher and his loyal hard-working crew.

A bitter-sweet moment. Their Salvage Rights validated. Their search areas defined and enforced by the Court. The search for the Atocha's Mother Lode was now impeded only by time, strong currents, fierce weather and thick layers of shifting sand covering the shipwreck's scattered treasure.

One of Fisher's salvage ships, The Tug Boat Northwind, Captained by Mel's son Dirk, anchored for the night of July 19th, 1975 near the Marquesas, thirty miles from Key West. A conventional three-story high Tug Boat, the Northwind was top-heavy, maintaining stability by equalizing the weight of diesel oil in port and starboard fuel tanks. The boat's Trim was controlled by a fuel transfer valve safety-wired shut when not underway.

At Key West that morning, a rubber toilet fitting connected to the bilge pump failed, flooding the engine room, causing Northwind to list precariously to starboard. Replaced and tested, the fitting seemed reliable as the Tug headed out for the Marquesas.

With harrowing legal issues resolved, and the Marquesas's sands now yielding tantalizing clues to the location of the Mother Lode, the eleven happy shipmates aboard the Northwind celebrated more than Angel Fisher's 28th birthday that night. After seven arduous years, the goal they sought seemed within reach. They turned in early. Tomorrow promised to be another hopeful day.

With only six bunks below deck, five crew members moved mattresses topside and slept under the stars unaware the toilet fitting had failed again, flooding the engine room's starboard side. While they slept, the Northwind's top-heavy list to starboard slowly increased. Without warning from a bilge alarm, or a crewman standing watch that night, the sea was unforgiving.

Freeboard is the distance from a boat's waterline to the gunwales. Like many Tugboats, amidships, and aft, Northwind's freeboard was eighteen inches. As the starboard rail began submerging, the unsecured transfer valve on the port fuel tank opened. Thousands of gallons of oil suddenly shifted to the starboard tank. Despite a frantic effort to save the ship, the Northwind capsized, quickly sinking, trapping Dirk and Angel Fisher and Diver Rick Gage in their bunks. Sleeping below, 16 year old Kane Fisher, Donnie Jonas, and Jim Solanick managed to miraculously escape from the overturned hull. They had been suddenly awakened by an unknown voice shouting: - "We're taking on water!"

Treasure Salvor, Inc. never ran Navy-style taut ships. The Northwind and Vigilona's easy-going discipline signed-on and retained happy highly motivated hard-working crews that soon became a family of intimate friends. The sudden loss of three shipmates was devastating. It was months before they went to sea again.

And this was not their first loss. In May 1971, 22 year old Gary Borders, ignoring Fisher's restrictions against deep dives, descended to 240 feet using a tank rated for 30 minutes at a 30 foot depth. At 240 feet he had less than two minutes of air available. His body was never found. His diving buddy Rick Vaughn also ran out of air but managed to surface. Rushed to a decompression chamber he somehow survived a near fatal episode of the Bends. For the next fourteen years, fearing another tragedy, Fisher confined all searches to shallow waters. His divers permitted depths of no more than thirty feet. Ironically, it was not until his son Kim, in 1985, ignoring his father's restrictions finally located Atocha's Mother Lode at a depth of 53 feet.

Then in August 1973, a National Geographic photographer's son, 95 pound 11 year old Nicholas Littlehales, diving off the Southwind failed to quickly descend through a strong surface current and was sucked into the ship's propellers. Badly mangled, he died on arrival at the Boca Chica hospital.

Training SCUBA enthusiasts since 1950, Mel emphasized prudent judgment, a Buddy system where safety-conscious Divers never dived alone. Not anticipated by his curriculum were the hazards of faulty fuel transfer valves and failed toilet fittings. Shielding Southwind's propellers with man-proof cages and restricting all dives to shallow waters, Mel did all he could to insure his crew's safety knowing the most friendly sea can be a bad master. The day of the Northwind disaster he commented: - "My son is dead, and I accept that. It's a powerful ocean; it takes men and ships."

With five dead searching for the Mother Lode, the cruelty of his loss was intensified by critical stories about Mel's "pathological obsession". "How many more victims to Fisher's greed would The Curse of The Atocha claim?" was typical. All the past scandal-mongering and personal animosity evoked by the media revived. And most painful were Lawsuits by Rick Cage and Angel Fisher's family. At this low point in his quest, Fisher's resilience enabled him to continue raising money, searching for solutions to his intractable problems, sustaining morale with never-failing confidence. If Kirk's death was to have meaning the quest for the Atocha must not be abandoned.

Fortunately there were several men respecting and admiring Mel Fisher who made his ultimate success possible. Eugene Lyon, Director of the St. Augustine Foundation was a dedicated researcher of Florida's Hispanic beginnings. A remarkable Historian, his head and heart lived in the 16th century. At the Archive of the Indies, in Seville, Spain, Lyon studied ancient shipwrecks. Information recorded in Atocha's Manifests, Logs, and Journals, shared with Fisher, located a promising search area in the Marquesas off Key West providing positive identification of the Spanish Galleon. Marine Archeologist Duncan Mathewson joined Treasure Salvors to photograph and map all excavation sites identifying and recording recovered artifacts. His disciplined scientific study of the wrecks refuted accusations by other critical Archeologists that Fisher's Divers were plundering historic sites, destroying a valuable national heritage.

A dedicated scientist, Mathewson worked honestly and imaginatively convinced that the knowledge derived from Mel's quest for Atocha's treasure was more valuable than the gold and would be useful to future scholars studying Hispanic-American history.

Another vital contributor to the successful salvage of the Atocha was Fay Field, an electronic genius who invented a portable magnetometer capable of detecting metal objects underwater. Towed over the sea bottom, his magnetometer identified "anomalies"; sites deviating from normal background readings. For sixteen years, "Magging" the bottom in a forty mile long by six mile wide area, marking "anomalies" with buoys, then diving after removing layers of sand to uncover the site, visually examined untold miles of ocean floor.

The search concentrated on an area adjacent to the Marquesas, thirty eight miles from Key West. The Quicksands. Shallow and safe. Mel's intuitive choice.

Boats towing the "Mags" maintained predetermined tracks over the bottom with Transit Theodolites, surveying instruments measuring vertical and horizontal angles. At stationary platforms adjacent to the search area, observors used Theodolites to instantly signal course deviations to the towing boat.

For sixteen years thousands of "anomalies" were located, uncovered, dived on and visually identified. Difficult and hazardous work. The area was also a Navy bombing range littering the ocean floor with ordinance that appeared as "anomalies" on the magnetometers. Before Divers could identify them, thick layers of sand were removed by deflecting propeller "prop wash" downward, creating Blow Holes, six foot wide craters uncovering the coral sea bed.

Attached to the stern of salvage ships, mail-box shaped deflectors directed powerful surges of water at the bottom blowing away tons of heavy sand. Day after day, under a hot sun, in fair weather and foul, the search routine continued. Heart-breaking drudgery. "Magging" along pre-determined tracks, marking "anomalies" with buoys, creating Blow Holes before diving to visually determine what had been uncovered became a heart-breaking process of repeated failure searching for "The Bitch Galleon of the Sea" -- The Atocha.

The salvage crews were isolated from shore and often short of food. Their only recreation spearfishing to relieve a monotonous diet. To conserve fuel they remained anchored at dive sites for weeks enduring discomfort with remarkable good will. Being at sea can be addictive. Soon they became hooked on shipboard life as they pursued a dream of finding Atocha's Mother Lode.

Mel's almost paranoid fear of the dangers involved in deep water diving limited his crew's to depths under thirty feet. Ignoring contrary advice he insisted the Mother Lode would be found in shallow water. Risking lives elsewhere would be foolish. Unnecessary.

Dirk and Kane Fisher believed the Atocha wreck lay in the depths south of the Quicksands. In the fall of 1984, ignoring Mel's restrictions, Kane redirected several unsuccessful "Magging" searches away from the shallow Quicksands into deeper water. Whenever possible, he continued to search forbidden depths until on July 18th 1985, after 16 years of coming up empty in shallow water, Kane Fisher located the Atocha's Mother Lode at a depth of 53 feet.

More than six hundred delighted investors and employees were now given their carefully calculated share of recovered treasure. Unhappily the gold, silver, emeralds, doubloons and valuable artifacts distributed were not readily convertible to cash. Real spending money could only come from Collectors and Museums purchasing the Atocha treasure in an over-stocked buyer's market. Suddenly wealthy, but cash poor, unable to pay their income taxes assessed in the 50 per cent bracket, after 16 years of privation, danger and dedication many felt having their great dream come true was no great bargain.

And some, unprepared for living an unexciting life after the hunt for the Atocha ended, feeling emotionally spent, were often self-destructive. Several of Mel's burned-out crews turned to drugs and alcohol to ease their disappointment. Deprived of constant danger and the stimulation of an adrenaline high - Life seemed empty. Hardly worth living.

Some men can not live without a dream. And there are a few extraordinary individuals, endowed by intelligence and imagination who make dreams possible. Mel Fisher was neither a Pied Piper or a Con Man exploiting the gullibility of dreamers. When he sustained the hopes and expectations of investors and crews proclaiming "Today is the day!" he truly believed everything he promised. So great was the power of his belief, so intense his conviction, so persuasive his personal dedication, few could resist a personal invitation to join his hazardous quest.

Mel was a Leader. Like the Pathfinders guiding the Covered Wagons across the prairie to California and Oregon promising free land and a richer life, he was distinct. Different. Striving to be what no one else could be. To those who believed and risked their lives with him, he was a Hero. A great Leader who shared their risks. A man who really stood up for what he believed holding himself accountable, becoming larger than himself. Larger than life.

Unfortunately, frustrating our need for Heroes there is a savage effort to tear down, trash, destroy and humiliate anyone who rises above the crowd.

Mel Fisher was such a man. In December 1998, with his ashes floating on the waters above the Atocha, his family, friends and other participants in his quest shed few tears. It seemed that Mel did not die. His great dream of finding fabulous amounts of treasure will somehow never end.

In December, 2003, when sailing the Florida Keys, I questioned an attractive, intelligent woman about Mel Fisher. "Yes", she replied. "I know all about that Chicken Farmer!" Her contempt and disdain confirmed that eighteen years after finding the Atocha's Mother Lode trashing Fisher's good name continues. Many still deny his integrity and achievement.

In our media-driven culture of personal destruction we have lost our are ability to separate media hype from truth. In 24 hour seven day a week news cycles rumor, unfounded allegations, libel and outright lies are sensationally reported as fact. Rigorous fact-checking by professional journalists are an exception rather than a rule we once relied on.

Nations perish for lack of reliable sources of truth. Today, our media have been given enormous power over our future. By silence, by accepting pervasive mendacity as an integral aspect of our culture in government, journalism, business, education and religion we have given our consent to being told lies. By accepting the trashing of reputations we say one man's good name does not matter. The truth about one individual is of no account.

Honest citizens can be a called Con Men, Chicken Farmers, or Enemy Combatants and the pejorative label is accepted and validated by our refusal to question the accusation. If you see it in print or on TV it must be true, too many believe.

"Truth shall make thee Free," said Chaucer in his Ballad of Good Counsel advising that without a decent regard for Truth, Freedom will surely perish.

And without Freedom, our sense of national community vanishes. Enraged Americans are now fighting fellow Americans. Preying on each other with words that instigate violence. Our political divisions multiply far beyond all previous partisanship, separating group from group,neighbor from neighbor, friend from friend. Citizen from immigrant. "One nation, indivisible,with Liberty and Justice for all" may indeed become, an impossible dream.

A RECURRING DREAM

I dream I am on Kuai, Hawaii's most isolated and primitive island hiking the black volcanic sand beach along the Pali coast where I encounter Bernard, the brother I lost at the close of the second world war. He is tanned, healthy, quietly reserved, not at all delighted to see his younger brother after an absence of many years.

"What are you doing here?" I ask. "Why didn't you come home?"

He shakes his head. Smiles his familiar enigmatic smile that is never sad or happy, turns and walks away.

I follow. Ask again. Demanding. "What the hell are you doing here? Why didn't you come home?"

He stops, turns and faces me. No longer smiling. For a moment I believe he is glad I'm here. We once were very close. Bonded. Truly brothers.

"I didn't want to come home, he says quietly."

I can not restrain my anger. Shouting. "Don't you know what you did? Don't you know about Mom? Dad will never be the same! Don't you know how I felt? Your death destroyed our family."

217

"Yes," he replies. I can imagine what you all went through.

"You selfish bastard," I screamed. He stepped back, retreating from my fury surprised at my anger.

"I am sorry," he says. Turns and strolls down the beach. I run after him. "The hell with your sorry," I shout. "The hell with your sorry and the hell with you."

Bernard stops, turns, opening his arms as if to embrace me. A familiar loving gesture. "Calm down," he says in a gentle voice. "Calm down," he says smiling. "I did what I had to do. I couldn't come home."

I struggle to control my fury. I can hardly speak. I ask, pleading, "you gave up coming home and living the life that could have been yours, for this?" I shout, pointing at the vacant barren beach. "You abandoned your loving family for this emptiness?" I say again.

"Yes," he replied. "Yes."

"Do you have any idea of the rich full life you missed?" I ask.

"Yes. I know what I have missed," he says. "I know what I have avoided."

I hesitate. Searching for a compelling answer. "Avoided? I reply. What you avoided is Life itself. Living."

"Yes," he answers. "That's what death is. The opposite of being alive."

"Come home, come home, I plead. Come home before it is too late."

"Come home to what?" Bernard says, shaking his head. Pausing. He turns and faces me. "Come home to grief and strife? Pain and anger? Struggling for the almighty dollar? Come home to ambition and depression? Success and failure? Mortgages and debts and all the other crap you call living the good life. That's not for me. Not for me. No way."

"You are a god damn coward," I shout.

"That's right. That's right." He replies. "A coward. A happy coward." He turns and strolls down the beach.

I do not follow. Say no more. Abandon my hopes. Allow this final image of my brother to fade from sight. Disappear down the beach. With the roar of the surf pounding in my ears I awaken.

In 1946, losing my brother Bernard as a result of wartime injuries, my father also lost his dream of having a son inherit the engineering business he established in 1920. My pre-war struggles as an engineering student, and my personal creative ambitions made clear I was a reluctant candidate for the job even though during high school holidays and weekends I enjoyed working as an electrician's assistant, meter tester and reader, bill collector, and draftsman.

The intense feeling of joyous freedom I experienced after leaving the Navy and returning to college on the GI Bill, was but a memory. I no longer felt free to go anywhere and do anything I pleased. As a surviving son of grieving parents I had acquired serious family responsibilities. Enjoying unlimited command of my life now seemed an empty dream.

At twenty one, was the life I wanted over? Was I no longer free to choose my future? Along with my responsibility to others, had I no responsibility to myself? To who and what I was? To my gifts and talents? To what I needed to live a full, productive and creative life that was truly my own life?

Which dream was I to follow? I admired my father's ambition to pass on to his sons his hard-won success. As a child of the depression years I recognized the lifetime security he offered would be his life's greatest achievement. And did I have the right to deny him his dream? For my father to lose both a son and a dream seemed unacceptable. Cruel.

By the end of that tragic summer I worked out the answer to these questions. I had my dreams. Vague feelings about who I was and what I contained. A chaotic inner surge of ambitions I could not deny without losing the greatest of all freedoms. The freedom to be myself. Dartmouth's Thayer School of Engineering lost a reluctant student - while I acquired a life I could truly call my own.

MY FATHER'S DESK

Uncluttered. Disciplined. Like his mind. Arranged precisely on a dark oak desktop; a small writing pad, a green tinted lamp and miniature sword letter-opener. My Father's desk. Sanctuary in a small back room in a home never at rest with a servant incessantly vacuuming, dusting and picking up after three boisterous children unsupervised by a mother forever on a telephone that interrupted meals with predictable frequency.

A floor-to-ceiling bookcase covered one wall of Dad's Study forbidden territory when he was home. Do not knock, do not enter permitted no exceptions when the door was closed and when Dad wasn't playing the violin he read. The complete works of Dickens, Poe, Kipling, and Robert Louis Stevenson in leather bound sets filled the upper shelves. On a lower shelf his Brooklyn Polytech college textbooks memorialized past achievements. "The mind has mountains" he said proudly, "and I climbed them." To his sons, these books confirmed an education diligently acquired in evening classes. On lower shelves, accessible to children, sets of The Book of Knowledge

221

and an Encyclopedia Britannica shared space with rows of novels of Walter Scott, Fenmore Cooper, Mark Twain, and my beloved Booth Tarkington's Penrod and Sam series. My introduction to childhood rebellion. At random on other shelves were currently popular novels and non-fiction; - John Steinbeck, Sinclair Lewis, Pearl Buck, John Roy Carlson and the incisive Dorothy Thompson who described a world moving out of a great depression into an even greater war. For three golden hours between school and dinner, I had access to this absorbing realm of joyous imagination and frightening reality. Passing through that open door of my Father's Study at an early age I quickly emerged from my privileged and sheltered childhood. My Rite of Passage traversed a human landscape where I found love and hate, Good and Evil, the sanctity of life, and the inevitability of death.

From 1936 to 1939 the probability of another World War was obvious. Hitler's Rhineland occupation, the Austrian Anschluss, the Munich Agreement and the German/Soviet alliance dominated headlines and radio news broadcasts. Krystalnacht, "The Night of the Broken Glass", and then the surrender of France confirmed our worst fears. As did one afternoon in June 1940, a hot, bright day shimmering with adolescent expectations when I stepped into a BMT subway car at the 28th street and Broadway station and entered a domain of doom and gloom. I did not understand why the usual crowd of exhausted passengers seemed in a state of shock. Almost dazed. I looked around. Puzzled. Seated, or standing, crowded together, many had tears in their eyes. Several stifled sobs. Looking over the shoulder of an elderly man I saw the front page photo of the New York Daily News. German troops marching under the Arc de Triumph in Paris. Another reminder that something irreversible and terrible has happened to a world that was too much with us. Too much with me. I could not turn off, tune out or ignore what was happening on the other side of the Atlantic.

The Philco AM radio on the night table next to my bed had a Short Wave Band. With the volume turned low, my bedroom door closed, the eleven o'clock BBC News of the Day reported the heroic Battle of Britain and tragic bombing of London, Coventry and Liverpool. Night after night, week after week, all summer and fall I heard flat monotone English accented voices describe a titanic struggle between Good and Evil with the outcome very much in doubt.

A Stamp Collection provided relief from this turmoil. This obsession with news matched my passion for collecting and then trading postage stamps with classmates. My reach was world wide. Rare and colorful stamps from China, Japan, and Thailand. Portraits of Latin American Liberators like Bolivar and Marti and pastoral scenes from Africa were much in demand by envious friends and a source of great pride and some income for me.

One winter evening in 1939 my father walked into my room and handed me an envelope. Before I could question him he vanished into his Study and closed the door. I studied the unsealed envelope a moment trying to guess what it contained and certainly with no idea of what impact it would have on my ambivalent feelings for my father. I opened the flap and poured out a cascade of postage stamps, some attached to scraps of envelopes they were torn from. Delighted, I arranged them in neat mounds. Hungary. Austria. Czechoslovakia. Poland. Germany. A collection of heroic portraits: Hungary's Admiral Horthy, The Czech President Jan Masaryk, Poland's General Pilsudski. And to my dismay, a Swastika stamp and portraits of Adolf Hitler. One as a Knight in bright armor on a white horse.

Where? How? Why? What was my father doing in the solitude of his room? How did he acquire these stamps? Obviously more was happening in his sanctuary than reading and playing the violin. But why the mystery? Why did he not explain the source of these stamps? All of them from Europe at war.

After school one rainy afternoon I entered his room to find a book. Steinbeck's *Grapes of Wrath* had just arrived in the mail. Walking in I brushed past a waste basket and accidently tipped it over. I knelt to pick up the trash scattered on the rug. Five or six envelopes addressed to my father. The upper right corners, where the postage stamps should be, torn off. My interest in Steinbeck aborted. On the upper left corner of the envelopes, return addresses confirmed the source of my father's surprising gift. But what did he do with the letters mailed to our home in these discarded envelopes?

His desk drawers, previously off-limits to my curiosity, held the answer. In our home we did not read each other's mail, examine school bags, or ask intrusive questions. Trust and respect for privacy were inviolable.

An overpowering need to know vanquished my sense of shame and guilt and like the Biblical apple devoured by Eve the upper left drawer of my father's desk taught me my first lesson about the dire consequences of knowledge. Of knowing only something about a complicated subject. "A little knowledge is a dangerous thing" - was a saying I often heard but failed to understand. Opening the drawer I found many letters in English in precise and attractive script. Clipped to the letters were photographs. Young men. Youths. Hair combed. Neckties straight. All smiling expectantly at the camera like photographs in a high school Yearbook. Some were my age. Bright piercing eyes I could not turn away from.

The letters stated height, weight, health, education, age, personal references and a brief description of their families. All sought a U.S. Visa with a guarantee of financial responsibility by a sponsor.

I read the letters. Requests from Germany, Austria, Hungary and Czechoslovakia filled the drawer until September 1939 when Germany invaded Poland and legal emigration ended. I knew nothing then about the futile guarantees my father mailed to Washington each one disregarded by the bigoted Breckenridge Long of the State Department denying tens of thousands of Visa applications condemning to death a generation of young Jews no older than myself.

As an avid reader of the NY Times I did know about the Ocean Liner St. Louis and several thousand Jewish Emmigrants with invalidated Cuban Visas denied entry at Havana. For several weeks I followed their futile attempt to gain permission to land in Mexico or Miami. Public indifference seemed to support bureaucratic anti-semitism. Then the unbelievable happened. Without Visas for their desperate passengers, the St Louis returned to the city it departed three months ago, Hamburg Germany.

Jews condemned to an unimaginable fate for want of a valid Visa. I became intensely aware that this drawer filled with letters and photographs contained the gift of life itself. A gift I believed was in my father's power to bestow. His apparent indifference, or lack of response to these requests stoked the fires of my adolescent anger.

One letter and photograph haunted me. I looked at it whenever I opened the drawer. A boy, my age, writing an attractive and disciplined script that shamed my handwriting. A somehow familiar face. Hair parted on one side. Smooth cheeks. Head turned, eyes raised to stare into the camera. Proud. Almost defiant. With no suggestion of a fugitive fleeing for his life.

Staring at that photograph evoked an intense desire to know his fate. I dared not ask and disclose my surreptitious entry into my father's desk. After a few months, as the drawer filled I again retrieved that letter and photograph from the bottom of the pile.

My compassion for the boy became an unreasoning anger at my father's failure to rescue someone who I now recognized looked like myself. Same eyes. Hair. Chin. He even smiled a little. Like I did when troubled.

In December 1940, the seven o'clock CBS radio news transmitted Edward R. Murrow's harrowing "This is London Calling" broadcasts. London was not only calling, it was burning and Murrow's vivid descriptions added to my fear for the future evoked by LIFE magazine's photographs of the devastation of Warsaw and Rotterdam. It seemed no force on earth could resist the triumph of Hitler's satanic will. Charles Lindberg, my childhood hero, and other isolationists crowded Madison Square Garden to keep America out of the war. The German Consul held a Victory dinner at the Waldorf attended by all the top executives of American industry eager to do business with Hitler's New Order that now seemed inevitable.

I felt I had to do more than feel sorry for the boy in that haunting photograph. I had not read Sigmund Freud. I knew nothing about guilt feelings. Transference. Over-identification. Oedipus complexes and other terms derisively called psychobabble. What I did know was that I was angry. Outraged. And most of this fury was directed at my father's apparent denial of the disaster described every morning in the New York Times.

One outlet for my anger was borrowing and then joyriding a neighbor's car. The father of my closest friend Leonard Lebow regularly went to bed no later than nine PM. Night after night we rolled his large green four door Packard down the driveway into the street and for the next two hours toured Brooklyn and Queens and Long Island's Sunrise Highway.

At fifteen, we were both more than six feet tall appearing older than our age and with England's defeat imminent we began talking about enlisting.

Canada beckoned. Many Americans had crossed the border to volunteer. Why not us? As we parked the car in the driveway that night we agreed to hitch-hike to Montreal the next morning. The Canadian Air Force desperately needed pilots and we were eager to learn to fly.

Our great adventure began at dawn on the BMT subway to Times Square where we transfered to the

IRT and rode to the end of the line at Yonkers. A short Trolley ride brought us to the Ferry Boat landing where we crossed the Hudson to Alpine New Jersey. US Route 9W according to our road map led North to Montreal. We waited on the side of the highway, rucksacks stuffed with Ponchos, sleeping bags, food, and some clothing soon to be discarded for uniforms. We raised our thumbs and in high spirits were off to war.

The Good Samaritans carrying us on our way were my first experience with the open minded generosity and instant good will of ordinary people. Truck drivers. Traveling salesman. Farmers. Delivery men. Migrant workers. They stopped. Offered us rides, eager for company. And then they talked. Each with an interesting story to tell. Route 9W on the west shore of the Hudson ran through the center of Haverstraw, Newburgh, Kingston, Catskill, and Albany providing a panorama of what America looked like and how it worked and lived. Thruways and Interstates today can not possibly offer that education.

A midnight meal at "Sy's" Diner outside Kingston offered us a choice of our next ride. Lonely, isolated, wanting someone to talk to, long-haul truckers welcomed two young kids from Brooklyn heading north to enlist. "I'd do the same," one said, "if I didn't have a family to support."

After gorging ourselves on scrambled eggs, hash brown potatoes and buttered toast the friendly Trucker picked up the check and offered to take us to Lake George, gateway to the Adirondacks.

He warned about the wilderness ahead. There would be little traffic between the lake and Platsburgh and a ride carrying us all the way was essential. We waited for hours at a Diner just outside of town studying weary Truckers hunched over coffee cups, eyes half-closed, chain smoking and then hopefully heading North.

At the far end of the counter a driver flirted with a young waitress. I turned and listened. He was speaking French. I waited as his romantic overtures were rebuffed. Laughing, the waitress filled his coffee cup, turned and walked off with a provocative wiggle. The driver shrugged and looked at me as I approached. "Excusez-moi," I said in my best Brooklyn-accented French acquired after one year at James Madison High. "Excusez-moi," I repeated as the startled driver grinned and shook his head. "Excusez-moi?" he laughed, exaggerating my accent. Then in perfect English said: "What you mean is you want a ride and you think I'm a dumb Canuck?"

I nodded, gesturing at Leonard watching us from the other end of the counter. "He with you?" he asked. Again I nodded. "Well hop in and don't stop talking. I warn you. I haven't slept in two days."

All the way to Montreal, despite our fears, he remained awake. We listened and he did all the talking relating a snapshot picture of French Canada. Eight brothers and sisters. Ageing parents living alone. Impoverished small villages abandoned by the young searching for work. As a matter of fact he told us proudly, he was the only one in his family with a job. He supported them all.

In Montreal at the intersection of St. Catherine East and Peel street we said goodby and "merci beaucoup" to our exhausted driver who for the final hour of our journey spoke French. The Canadian

Air Force Recruiting Office was just up the street he explained and with an encouraging wave and a "Bonne chance!" he drove off, his destination home and bed.

The recruiting sergeant seated behind a desk did not smile as we entered. We'd been awake for two days. Unwashed, hair uncombed, carrying rucksacks. He knew who we were and where we came from. Unpromising candidates in a long parade of hopeful under-age warriors in need of a bath and a good night's sleep. He gestured at chairs and we sat down. He handed us enlistment papers and pencils and silent and watchful as a cat watched as we filled out the long forms. Just above our signature was date of birth, abbreviated DOB.

We added two years and signed our names.

The sergeant was in no rush. Slowly, line by line, he studied the forms alternately looking at us and nodding his head as we sweated our future.

He put the papers down, leaned back in his chair and smiled. I thought, an encouraging smile. Hopefully a welcoming smile. The sergeant was a big man. Bulging his uniform. Face flushed by years of food and drink. His eyes clear. Intent. Questioning. Then he tilted his head back and laughed. A full, good-natured, unrestrained laugh that somehow lightened the burden of our disappointment. "Byes," he said, in a happy lilted brogue, "Cum beck an see me when y'er a bit more dry behind the ears!"

The return of the prodigal sons was uneventful. A fierce snowstorm at Platsburgh ruled out hitchhiking. With enough money for two Greyhound Bus tickets, a cup of coffee and a sandwich we fell into our seats and slept all the way to New York to be greeted with indifference by our families who never doubted our return. My father did not speak to me for several months. My mother asked a few questions. Amused. Her sense of fun and adventure somehow aroused.

Two years later, Leonard enlisted in the Marines and died in the Pacific on some island unknown to me. After graduating Madison High School that June my classmates and I scattered and lost contact as we enlisted or were drafted. With one exception our families were not acquainted and it was not until four years later in October 1945 that I learned what had become of my friends.

Following several semesters at Dartmouth the summer and fall of 1942 I enlisted as a Naval Aviation Cadet and after my release from the Navy in October 1945 returned to my High school to say hello to my favorite teachers. I also wished to show I had come back from the war, alive and well, and was happy to see them.

To my surprise mounted on a wall in the lobby a large wooden panel displayed the names of former students serving in the military and Merchant Marine. After locating my name I studied the panel searching for my classmates' names. At first I did not realize what I was seeing. Gold Stars next to so many names. Gold Stars?

I was stunned when I realized I was looking at the names of friends killed in France, Germany, England, and the Pacific. Ten names. One, Wilbur Goldsmith, died in a Meningitis epidemic on a Troopship coming home from France. Bob Nassau who gave up a four year Harvard Scholarship, shot down over the Mediterranean, and Sol Tyson in the Battle of the Bulge. And Herb Lerner of the Eight Air Force, now buried in a Military Cemetery in Cambridge, England. Overwhelmed, I quickly walked out of the school, my happy social visit aborted.

At that time no funerals or rituals of mourning allowed me to grieve. There was no closure. It was as if between 1942 and 1945 my friends and classmates had vanished. Disappeared. Never existed. And, to my shame I held on to my happiness at being alive and returning to college. In fact, that evening, I saw my favorite Broadway show, "Carousel" enjoying the company of a very interesting young lady.

Two years before in the cold and blustery winter of 1943 my mother rode a day coach to Indiana where I was learning to fly at Bunker Hill Naval Air Station sixty miles north of Indianapolis. At dinner that evening in the Hotel Lincoln's dining room she told me of the death of a friend and neighbor Herbert Lerner killed returning to his base in England. Herb was the son of Rose Lerner, my mother's High school classmate and to her surprise I asked no questions. Could not share her great sense of loss. I'm sure she thought my behavior unfeeling. Cold.

Then, fifty seven years later, watching a televised memorial service for the USS Cole sailors killed by terrorists in Yemen I broke down. The years of distancing myself from past sorrows dissolved in a sob. I could not stop the tears. And with my tears came a great sense of release as I realized I was now at last attending funerals I missed in 1945. Indeed this eruption of sorrow included my older brother whose funeral service I also missed.

Names and faces. Faces and names. They come alive as we remember them. Basic emotions are with us forever. Years of denial and repression, callous indifference can not suppress our deepest and most profound feelings. We are what we feel as well as what we think and fifty seven years could not erase a single moment of my pain.

DACHAU

In 1979 while working in Munich, and with a day off, I rented a car and drove to Dachau. Outside the concentration camp I parked in a lot that could accommodate several thousand cars and buses. The camp, the museum, and three religious memorials are crowded tourist attractions complete with souvenir postcards. At Dachau, the Gas Chamber, the Gallows, and the Crematoria are adjacent to, but outside the perimeter of the main camp reached by a narrow foot bridge crossing over a water-filled moat and passing through a high voltage electrified barbed-wire fence.

In this separate area, one hundred yards from a brick building housing the Gas Chamber and the Crematoria, there is a large circular mound of human ashes, about thirty feet in diameter and twenty feet high. In the center of this mass grave is a small, flat stone inscribed with the Star of David. Leading away from this memorial is a narrow footpath winding through a small grove of Pine trees. A dense, dark woods. Certainly haunted though carefully maintained, looking more like a park than a forest.

Following this path, through these woods, you walk past other burial mounds, each with an identifying footstone; a Cross, a Star of David, or a small sign indicating where among these trees mass executions occurred. There was also a small glade, or open area in the forest, with a wooden bench for visitors to rest while contemplating the horrors described in neatly lettered signs in six languages.

Circling through this forest, following this footpath, you pass more mass graves, each marked by religion or nationality, emerging from the woods to your starting point, the large burial mound of ashes with the large Star of David.

As if timed to my return, two Groundskeepers wearing spotless blue coveralls walked out of a nearby Tool shed and began raking the area. There was not a stray leaf, or a scrap of paper, or a discarded cigarette to be seen anywhere.

The large burial mound was also entirely bare. Other than the Star of David in the center, there was not a stone, not a pebble. How could this be?

There is a traditional practice of placing a small stone, or a pebble as a token of a visit to a Jewish grave. Certainly for more than forty years, thousands of relatives or friends visited this site. So where were the memorial stones?

I was also certain that two old Groundskeepers, raking with all their might could not clear this area. No! Not in a thousand years! So where were the stones?

A perplexing question awakening within me long dormant feelings. A religiosity ignored or denied by many years of quiescent non-observance. I realized at that moment, understanding the emotions that once were so intense in my childhood, would be like searching for those missing stones.

All I had to do was open my eyes.

The stones were everywhere.

I was surrounded by stones.

I was standing on stones.

The entire perimeter around the mass grave was covered with thousands of small stones. Different shapes. Different colors. Pebbles. Little fragments. Rocks.

Each one, no matter how small, now matter how insignificant, marked the visit of someone, coming to this sacred place, to this mound of human ashes, to acknowledge and revive a Faith that has proven to be, for five thousand years, as indestructible as stone.

BROOKLYN

During the bitter cold winter of 1932 I learned about our turbulent world from newspaper headlines and radio broadcasts describing the evils of Prohibition, Bootlegging, and The Great Depression. Vivid stories about hunger and unemployment rivalled news about President Hoover's inability to reduce crime or repair our demoralized economy.

My participation in these events began when my father sent me to Barash's Pharmacy to pick up his weekly medical Prescription. Doc Barash, a Registered Pharmacist, was best known for stitching wounds and setting broken limbs while reassuring mothers that the inevitable accidents of childhood were rarely fatal. That Doc Barash was also known for selling Bootleg whiskey only added to his reputation for public service that continued long after FDR's election in 1933 repealed unenforceable Prohibition Laws.

Every Saturday morning with five dollars in my pocket I bicycled to Barash's Pharmacy on Nostrand Avenue and with a brown paper bag strapped in my carrier basket returned home with an illegal cargo of "Old Overholt", "Three Feathers", or "Johnny

Walker" whiskey. Or so the counterfeited labels said. It never occurred to me I had become a Rum Runner, a child eluding the police, a part of the crime epidemic spawned by Prohibition Laws everyone ignored.

From Kings Highway to Quentin Road East 28th street was one of Brooklyn's more affluent residential neighborhoods attracting many unemployed men wandering from door to door offering to mow lawns, tend furnaces, take out ash barrels, or wash windows in exchange for a meal or hopefully a dollar or two.

My mother never said "No" to these requests often devising tasks enabling her to provide meals in exchange for work. Our windows were often washed several times a week. The furnace fueled several times a day without a hint of charity being given or received. The men appearing at our back door were polite, doing their assigned chores and eating the meals they earned without any sense of shame. "There but for the Grace of God go any one of us" was my mother's reaction to these unfortunate but still proud men.

With the advent of President Roosevelt's WPA Employment Programs in 1933 these requests for household work declined to two or three a week. The few men who did appear on East 28th street seemed to pass by our neighbors and go directly to 1682, our home. I was silent when my mother wondered why our address was the most popular Soup Kitchen on our street. Certainly her cabbage soup, hot coffee, and thick slices of Rye bread were no better than her neighbors.

Every weekday morning the BMT subway at Kings Highway brought us numerous street Vendors, door-to-door salesmen, and the unemployed hoping to earn a day's pay. Nearby, a block from the station, the 17th street Branch of the Brooklyn Public Library was my favorite after-school destination where I encountered many more interesting characters than those described in books. For some of the unemployed, weary after a day soliciting work, the Library provided a place to rest or read or gossip with anyone willing to answer their questions. When asked about a good place to find work I never hesitated to recommend my generous East 28th street neighbors specifying one who never turned anyone away. My mother.

But thanks to the jobs provided by FDR's WPA my career finding work for the unemployed soon aborted. I believe my mother may have discovered the reason for her reputation as Lady Bountiful - but she said not a word of praise or reproach.

My friend Eddie Rose lived in a big house on the corner of 28th street and Avenue P. A white Mediterranean Villa with a red tile roof. One of Brooklyn's more attractive homes. I often played with Eddie re-enacting in his backyard World War I battles with parallel rows of trenches manned by Eddie's army of toy soldiers. Flying miniature aeroplanes I bombed and strafed our make-believe battlefield imitating the rattle of machine guns and the roar of exploding bombs with my mouth. We took turns winning battles with a strong prejudice for the Allies vanquishing despicable Huns who everyone knew bayonetted Belgian babies before surrendering to our heroic General Pershing.

At the other end of East 28th street, at the corner of Quentin Road, once lived a Stock Broker who reacted to the 1929 Crash by falling out of his Wall Street office window. A tragedy never discussed after his family, our next door neighbor, lost their home and moved away.

In Eddie Rose's kitchen, however, I discovered a different reaction to financial disaster. Famished after hours of combat on the imaginary battlefields of France we went inside to raid the Ice Box. There, to my surprise, I noticed kerosene lanterns and candlesticks on a shelf and wondered why such old fashioned lights were still in use. Eddie laughed at my startled look and quickly explained his father had been wiped out in the Crash, and with bills unpaid, electricity had been turned off. In fact, he continued without embarrassment, the entire Rose family was living on Relief. That is, until his father found a job.

There, every evening, at the far end of East 28th street the warm yellow glow of candlelight flickered in the windows of Eddie Rose's home. The only house in the neighborhood without electric lights. A foreboding possibility Parents did not discuss with their children. For almost a year the Rose family struggled to hold on to their home and dignity with no hint of self pity or unhappiness. In fact playing war games with Eddie and visiting his large noisy family was fun. They were full of life and Eddie enjoyed much more freedom that I was ever permitted by my parents.

Then, one evening in 1934 the flickering candles in Eddie's windows were gone. Electricity has been turned on. The Rose's home was now no different from all the others on our street, windows brightly shining in the dark. Something to cheer about.

But not for me. I felt something important had been taken away from us. East 28th street had somehow changed in a way I did not understand. Years later, remembering that first night when my friend Eddie's electricity was restored I realized our neighborhood had lost something remarkable. A bright Beacon of hope and courage and family love had been extinguished except in my memory of those troubled years when in President Roosevelt's famous words: "The only thing we had to fear - was Fear itself."

To America's delight Walt Disney dramatized FDR's reassuring words by producing *The Three Little Pigs* animated cartoon with the song *Whose Afraid of The Big Bad Wolf* rivalling our national anthem in popularity. Soon the despairing song *Buddy Can You Spare A Dime* gave way to *Happy Days Are Here Again* as our nation's unquenchable optimism slowly revived.

However the childhood song I recall most vividly is *Needles and Pins, Needles and Pins, When a Girl marries her troubles begin* sung by a little old lady no more than five feet tall going from door to door with a tray of Needles, Pins, Buttons, Sewing Thread, Hair Ribbons, and other assorted household Notions.

Before Supermarkets and Malls were ever dreamed of convenient shopping for housewives was provided by street vendors such as the "Vegetable Man", a Truck Farmer from Long Island who drove along our street blowing his horn and boasting about his fresh lettuce, tomatoes, corn, and strawberries. He would then be followed by the "Ice Man" selling twenty five pound blocks of Ice, an "Old Clothes Man" buying and selling used clothes, "The Fuller Brush Man" and "The Hoover Man" selling Carpet Sweepers and Vacuum Cleaners. At least once a week "The Needles and Pins Lady" humming or singing that song rang our doorbell and my mother would dutifully buy a few items whether or not they were needed.

The Needles and Pins Lady often asked for a glass of water and permission to rest a moment on our front steps where unasked she would tell me about her family, her famous sons, the death of her husband and other imaginary events in her obviously unmarried and barren life.

She was likeable, cheerful, and with her Irish gift for story-telling always fascinating. But then, after several months selling to the housewives in our neighborhood she did not come again to East 28th street. No one knew her name or where she lived or whether she was ill or dead or perhaps peddling her "Notions" in another part of Brooklyn.

For me The Needles and Pins Lady will always be remembered whenever I hear her haunting words: "When a Girl Marries Her Troubles Begin. Needles and Pins. Needles and Pins."

After Hitler marched his Army into the Rhineland, occupied Austria and Destroyed Czechoslovakia, European politics commanded almost as much of my attention as Baseball. In 1938 with the humiliating Munich Agreement Hitler's future triumph over England and France seemed inevitable making it impossible to ignore what was happening Overseas. Confident in the ultimate victory of Nazi terror there emerged what my father called the "Lunatic Fringe". "The Silver Shirts", "The Christian Front", "The German-American Bund" and the followers of an anti-semitic Priest who broadcast every Sunday afternoon on a National Radio Network, "The Coughlinites".

Perched on Speaker's platforms on Kings Highway, flanked by American Flags and wearing military uniforms these purveyors of hate shouted and screamed their venomous doctrines imitating their Leader and Mentor Adolf Hitler. Der Fuehrer and Father of all the unhappy misfits and failures of the American gutter.

Only a few people stopped to listen. Most were window-shopping or going in and out of stores completely ignoring the insults and violent language of these "Nuts".

"It Can't Happen Here." "This is America." "Pay no attention and they'll go away" was the most common response to these hate-filled diatribes by my family, friends and neighbors most of whom were Jewish and should have felt more threatened.

Only Tony, our neighborhood's Italian Barber who for twenty-five cents could cut the hair of the most unruly child responded appropriately to these verbal assaults on human decency. "Fucka them!" he said as he ran a scissors and comb over my head. "Fucka alla them no good bastards."

Here was a man who made sense. Who felt as I did, particularly after a Christian Fronter set up his Flag and Speakers stand across the street from our Synagogue on Yom Kippur with a Policeman at his side to prevent trouble.

That this outrage was ignored by all the worshipers on that Holy day seemed cowardly. Unreal. And Tony agreed with me. "Someone should a breaka his head!" he said. "That's a the only way."

Visiting Tony's Barbershop was always fun. The semi-nude photographs in the "Police Gazette" and lurid stories in "True Adventure" magazine made waiting for a haircut an education in the forbidden underworld of sex and crime.

And now there was something more than adolescent curiosity to bring me to Tony's Barbershop.

"A Bassi Fascisti! A Viva Liberta!" Tony said.

"What's that?" I asked.

"Avanti Popolo!" Tony replied. "A song."

"What kind of song?" I asked again.

"Rivoluzione! Bandiera Rosa!" Tony explained.

"What my brother sang before the Fascisti killed him."

I said nothing. Tony was trimming around my ears with a straight razor. He was excited. I was afraid.

"They made him drink a gallon of Castor Oil so he should suffer before they beat him to death," he said.

Castor Oil? My father's favorite Laxative. Dispensed by the spoonful! A horrid taste even when diluted with orange juice. For Constipation a dose of Castor Oil was always prescribed. What torment.

"Horrible," I said. "Horrible."

"That's a right," Tony said. "That's a right! That's a why I aways say - Fucka them, Fucka them all!"

LESSONS LEARNED

I have been privileged to know, admire and learn from men and women who in my lifetime made America. I think of these "Makers of America" as heroic. Of fine character. Unimpeachable integrity. Many of them unknown, preferring anonymity to the vulgar celebrity that dominates today's culture. And looking back over the years, many significant learning experiences come to mind that influenced what I am today.

After every Navy training flight, Cadets gathered around Instructors for a "Lessons Learned" discussion that saved many lives. With every flight a learning experience, we acquired the self-confidence and skills needed to overcome flying's unforgiving challenges.

An so when coping with my life's unforgiving challenges, there were certain incidents and lessons that proved invaluable.

I have learned and believe there are certain laws that have not been annulled or repealed... Honor to family... loyalty to friends... respect for Law... love of country.

And that reason and morality, in the long run, will prevail, and that the use of force without diplomacy is doomed to failure.

I learned we can alleviate human suffering, injustice, and discrimination when we elect leaders determined to meet these challenges.

My childhood during the great depression confirmed this.

I saw proud men going from door to door asking to wash windows, take out garbage or stoke coal furnaces for a bowl of soup or a loaf of bread for their families. I learned compassion. "There but for the Grace of God go I."

At thirteen I saw the Dirigible "Von Hindenburg" circling Brooklyn before exploding in Lakehurst, N.J. and I understood the message conveyed by enormous Swastikas painted on the Dirigible's side. No ocean is wide enough to protect all who fled makers of Pogroms.

In 1938 I saw newsreel photos of "Krystalnacht", "The Night of the Broken Glass" when German synagogues were torched and my father told me "It can't happen here."

I was also outraged seeing the German American Bund, the Silver Shirts, and the Christian Front preaching hatred on the streets I walked to school every day.

In 1939 I followed the exciting drama of FDR and Churchill opposing Hitler with the outcome, Good versus Evil, unknown.

For years everyone I knew had Hitler on the brain. He was our "Frankenstein".

In 1939 I watched my father fill out Visa applications for friends and family hoping to flee

Europe. Life saving documents denied by our State Department's Breckinridge Long who stated: "We already have enough Jews here."

In 1940 I listened to Edward R. Murrow's "This is London" broadcasts reporting the "Blitz" adding to the horror evoked by Life Magazine photos of devastated Warsaw and Rotterdam.

In June 1940 I saw neighbors walking the streets dazed, sobbing over news photos of German soldiers marching under the Arc de Triumph the day France capitulated. That day, in Europe, only England remained free.

In 1941 I heard on the radio, the anti-semitic Father Coughlin and my childhood hero Charles Lindbergh describe "The Wave of The Future". The inevitable triumph of Hitler's "New Order" they said America must accept and do business with.

In 1942 I went off to war with twenty classmates. Eleven did not return. My brother also died of wartime injuries. I learned the high cost of freedom. Each death a family catastrophe recalled when I read the daily Body Count in the New York Times.

In 1945, thanks to the G.I. Bill of Rights I returned to Dartmouth with two memorable classmates; one Johnny Sirignano, blinded in France, graduated Dartmouth and Saint John's Law School, and despite his handicap became Federal District Attorney of New York. The other, our class Valedictorian, handsome Bob MacLeod, a B-17 pilot who survived facial burn disfigurement requiring years of corrective surgery. Two inspiring and unforgettable miracles of courage who taught me the true meaning of heroism and the importance of getting the most out of life despite horrific circumstances.

In 1946, I visited another classmate, bedridden at the Veterans Hospital on Kingsbridge Road, the Bronx, and learned that while I got the G.I. Bill other veterans, covered with bedsores, couldn't get their urine bags changed regularly.

In 1949, at a Screenwriter's Guild meeting in Hollywood to vote on support for the ten blacklisted screenwriters, I watched John Ford, a very conservative, patriotic American writer-director risk his career defending the freedom of men whose ideas he detested. I learned fear is contagious. That in a room filled with men worried about their careers, one brave voice can make a difference, can summon terrified citizens to fight for everyone's freedom of speech.

In 1951 I watched General Douglas MacArthur's triumphant return from Korea with a ticker-tape parade down New York's Fifth Avenue greeting a national hero who had been fired by President Harry Truman for insubordination. His "No substitute for victory" speech was cheered by Congress who welcomed him as a future Presidential candidate.

Then in 1952, at the Republican National Convention, I saw his ambitions collapse in humiliation when he received only one nominating vote. That day I learned our nation's ability to reject dangerous demagogues was alive and well in the U.S.A.

In 1952 I watched Senator Margaret Chase Smith of Maine, and Senator Flanders of Vermont, both Republicans, with an assist from lawyer Joseph Welch, end Senator McCarthy's reign of terror. Years when even President Eisenhower was intimidated.

In 1952 I wrote *Meet Clifford Case*, the campaign biography film for his successful run for the United States Senate. Republican Clifford Case was an ideal candidate with bi-partisan support. A Minister's son, endorsed by Labor Unions, with the promise of being an outstanding President, he abandoned politics after the unendurable slander of his sister who confessed to J. Edgar Hoover that she once was a Communist. I learned in the politics of personal destruction bad men drive good men out of government.

In 1961 I wrote and directed *The Next Step* a TV documentary dramatizing the elimination of Polio by Dr. Albert Sabin's more effective Oral vaccine. By heroic determination Dr. Sabin overcame powerful vested interests promoting the Salk vaccine which occasionally crippled children. Sabin's story is one of a dedicated researcher refusing to accept defeat by politically promoted inferior science.

In 1977 I wrote *Task Force 77* a TV documentary showing our Navy operating off the coast of Vietnam. Admiral Ralph W. Cousins the brilliant and handsome Task Force Commander invited me to dinner aboard his flagship where he expressed his dismay about public indifference to the fate of the POW's in Hanoi. With tears in his eyes he handed me the biographies he compiled on the POW's he once commanded. At a time when heartless Pentagon "Body Counts" of our casualties were a daily event, he assumed a more personal responsibility for their fate demonstrating leadership that truly valued the lives of all who served. An unforgettable lesson in humanity.

And finally, when working in countries where no one feels safe in the presence of his neighbors, where children receive medals for informing on parents, I learned how entire nations live in fear, passively accepting rule by small cliques of criminals. I acquired a greater appreciation of the freedoms we take for granted, the liberty we are sometimes too willing to sacrifice for national security.

Which brings to mind Benjamin Franklin's important lesson that: "They who would give up an essential liberty for temporary security, deserve neither liberty or security."

And unforgettably, Thornton Wilder's classic American play *Our Town* dramatized another lesson I have always known when he wrote:

"We all know that something is Eternal. And it ain't houses and it ain't names, and it ain't earth, and ain't even the stars.

"Everybody knows in their bones that something is Eternal, and that something has to do with human beings. There is something way down deep that is Eternal about every human being."

EPILOGUE

My beloved Oxford English Dictionary defines an Epilogue as "a section or speech at the end of a book or play serving as a comment on, or a conclusion to, what has happened."

Certainly my exuberant voyage has led to encounters with characters who helped me answer the self defining question: "Who am I?"

Meeting new people in new places in unusual circumstances provided invaluable insights that have been unpredictable, frustrating, frightening, and often heart breaking, though ultimately they have become the seeds of creativity.

Though the people in this memoir are gone, they live in memories that insure they will not perish again in a genocidal world that denies their existence.

When we recall and learn from the past, we affirm the possibility of a better future. And in writing about the past, I fulfill my obligation to all who shared with me the stories of their lives.

This memoir tells of a people "born in this century, tempered by war, disciplined by a hard and bitter peace, proud of our ancient heritage, willing to pay any price, bear any burden, meet any hardship, support any friend, oppose any foe to assure the survival and success of liberty."

In today's culture of mendacity, a passion for truth, ideas and literature seems old-fashioned. Quaint. Our manners, expectations and codes of behavior have been replaced by the today's televised lifestyles. "To thine own self be true," once a dominant moral imperative, has been replaced by "Greed is good" in mindless service to the "Bottom Line."

In 1968, filming the story of the Robert Kennedy inspired *Revitalization Corps*, I heard the assassinated President's brother say:

"What we need in the United States is not division; what we need in the United States is not hatred; what we need in the United States is not violence and lawlessness, but is love and wisdom, and compassion toward one another, and a feeling of justice toward those who still suffer within our country, whether they be white or whether they be black."

When Martin Luther King died, Robert Kennedy spoke out against "The mindless violence which again stains our land and every one of our lives... No wrongs have ever been righted by riots and civil disorders. A sniper is only a coward, not a hero; and an uncontrolled, uncontrollable mob is only the voice of madness, not the voice of reason."

He continued, saying: "Let us dedicate ourselves to what the Greeks wrote so many years ago: to tame the savageness of man and make gentle the life of this world. Let us dedicate ourselves to that, and say a prayer for our country and for our people."

Later Robert Kennedy expressed a hope for reconciliation: "Surely, we can learn, at least, to look at those around us as fellow men, and surely we can begin to work a little harder to bind up the wounds among us and to become in our own hearts brothers and countrymen once again."

Quoting George Bernard Shaw, Robert Kennedy summed up the spirit of optimism in his statement: "Some men see things the way they are, and ask why? I dream of things that never were, and ask why not?"

And so, at this moment in my exuberant voyage, I also ask: Why not? Why not dream of a saner world? Why not write books, essays, and memoirs hoping to transmit to readers the values I have received from so many others? Why not attempt to alter the murderous course of our history by refusing to join the pervasive complicity that is our silence?

Yes indeed, why not?

Author's Note

This memoir attempts to find meaning in the chaos of personal history. I am profoundly grateful to all who encouraged my effort to meet an obligation to bear witness. Above all, friend and author Lee Jacobus, whose wise counsel made publishing a work of memory possible.

About The Author

After a 42 year career as a writer-director of many Award-winning films and television programs, Norman Weissman has written two novels and a memoir. Determined to oppose the silence in which lies become history, the author makes his reply in art to tell of all he has witnessed during more than half a century of filming at home and overseas. He lives in rural Connecticut with his wife Eveline.

Also by Norman Weissman

"Acceptable Losses"
ISBN-13: 978-0-9801894-0-7

"Snapshots USA"
(An American Family Album)
ISBN-13: 978-0-9801894-1-4

www.ingramcontent.com/pod-product-compliance
Lightning Source LLC
Chambersburg PA
CBHW031830090426
42741CB00005B/195